MznLnx

Missing Links Exam Preps

Exam Prep for

Prealgebra

Bittinger & Ellenbogen, 4th Edition

The MznLnx Exam Prep is your link from the texbook and lecture to your exams.
The MznLnx Exam Preps are unauthorized and comprehensive reviews of your textbooks.

All material provided by MznLnx and Rico Publications (c) 2010
Textbook publishers and textbook authors do not particpate in or contribute to these reviews.

MznLnx

Rico
Publications

Exam Prep for Prealgebra
4th Edition
Bittinger & Ellenbogen

Publisher: Raymond Houge
Assistant Editor: Michael Rouger
Text and Cover Designer: Lisa Buckner
Marketing Manager: Sara Swagger
Project Manager, Editorial Production: Jerry Emerson
Art Director: Vernon Lowerui

Product Manager: Dave Mason
Editorial Assitant: Rachel Guzmanji
Pedagogy: Debra Long
Cover Image: Jim Reed/Getty Images
Text and Cover Printer: City Printing, Inc.
Compositor: Media Mix, Inc.

(c) 2010 Rico Publications

ALL RIGHTS RESERVED. No part of this work covered by the copyright may be reproduced or used in any form or by an means--graphic, electronic, or mechanical, including photocopying, recording, taping, Web distribution, information storage, and retrieval systems, or in any other manner--without the written permission of the publisher.

For more information about our products, contact us at:
Dave.Mason@RicoPublications.com

For permission to use material from this text or product, submit a request online to:
Dave.Mason@RicoPublications.com

Printed in the United States
ISBN:

Contents

CHAPTER 1
  WHOLE NUMBERS 1
CHAPTER 2
  INTRODUCTION TO INTEGERS AND ALGEBRAIC EXPRESSIONS 14
CHAPTER 3
  FRACTION NOTATION: MULTIPLICATION AND DIVISION 23
CHAPTER 4
  FRACTION NOTATION: ADDITION AND SUBTRACTION 32
CHAPTER 5
  DECIMAL NOTATION 37
CHAPTER 6
  INTRODUCTION TO GRAPHING AND STATISTICS 43
CHAPTER 7
  RATIO AND PROPORTION 51
CHAPTER 8
  PERCENT NOTATION 54
CHAPTER 9
  GEOMETRY AND MEASUREMENT 57
CHAPTER 10
  POLYNOMIALS 70
ANSWER KEY 80

TO THE STUDENT

COMPREHENSIVE

The *MznLnx* Exam Prep series is designed to help you pass your exams. Editors at MznLnx review your textbooks and then prepare these practice exams to help you master the textbook material. Unlike study guides, workbooks, and practice tests provided by the texbook publisher and textbook authors, *MznLnx* gives you **all** of the material in each chapter in exam form, not just samples, so you can be sure to nail your exam.

MECHANICAL

The MznLnx Exam Prep series creates exams that will help you learn the subject matter as well as test you on your understanding. Each question is designed to help you master the concept. Just working through the exams, you gain an understanding of the subject--its a simple mechanical process that produces success.

INTEGRATED STUDY GUIDE AND REVIEW

MznLnx is not just a set of exams designed to test you, its also a comprehensive review of the subject content. Each exam question is also a review of the concept, making sure that you will get the answer correct without having to go to other sources of material. You learn as you go! Its the easiest way to pass an exam.

HUMOR

Studying can be tedious and dry. MznLnx's instructional design includes moderate humor within the exam questions on occassion, to break the tedium and revitalize the brain

Chapter 1. WHOLE NUMBERS

1. In mathematics, a _____ is a number that can be expressed as an integral of an algebraic function over an algebraic domain. Kontsevich and Zagier define a _____ as a complex number whose real and imaginary parts are values of absolutely convergent integrals of rational functions with rational coefficients, over domains in given by polynomial inequalities with rational coefficients.
    a. Boussinesq approximation
    b. Disk
    c. Closeness
    d. Period

2. _____ is a numeral system in which each position is related to the next by a constant multiplier, a common ratio, called the base or radix of that numeral system.
    a. Negative base
    b. NegaFibonacci coding
    c. Cyrillic numerals
    d. Place value

3. A _____ number is a positive integer which has a positive divisor other than one or itself. By definition, every integer greater than one is either a prime number or a _____ number.zero and one are considered to be neither prime nor _____. For example, the integer 14 is a _____ number because it can be factored as 2 × 7.
    a. Composite
    b. Basis
    c. Key server
    d. Discontinuity

4. In mathematics, the _____ is a term used to describe the number of times one must apply a given operation to an integer before reaching a fixed point.

Usually, this refers to the additive or multiplicative persistence of an integer, which is how often one has to replace the number by the sum or product of its digits until one reaches a single digit. Because the numbers are broken down into their digits, the additive or multiplicative persistence depends on the radix.

   a. Linear congruence theorem
   b. Coprime
   c. Lychrel number
   d. Persistence of a number

5. In mathematics, a _____ can mean either an element of the set {1, 2, 3, ...} or an element of the set {0, 1, 2, 3, ...}. The latter is especially preferred in mathematical logic, set theory, and computer science.

Chapter 1. WHOLE NUMBERS

_____s have two main purposes: they can be used for counting, and they can be used for ordering.

a. Natural number
b. Strong partition cardinal
c. Cardinal numbers
d. Suslin cardinal

6. In mathematics, a _____ can mean either an element of the set {1, 2, 3, ...} (i.e the positive integers) or an element of the set {0, 1, 2, 3, ...} (i.e. the non-negative integers).

a. Bounded
b. FISH
c. Degrees of freedom
d. Whole number

7. In mathematics the concept of a _____ generalizes notions such as 'length', 'area', and 'volume'. Informally, given some base set, a '_____' is any consistent assignment of 'sizes' to the subsets of the base set. Depending on the application, the 'size' of a subset may be interpreted as its physical size, the amount of something that lies within the subset, or the probability that some random process will yield a result within the subset.

a. Cusp
b. Congruent
c. Measure
d. Lattice

8. _____ is the mathematical operation of scaling one number by another. It is one of the four basic operations in elementary arithmetic.

_____ is defined for whole numbers in terms of repeated addition; for example, 4 multiplied by 3 can be calculated by adding 3 copies of 4 together:

$$4 + 4 + 4 = 12.$$

_____ of rational numbers and real numbers is defined by systematic generalization of this basic idea.

a. The number 0 is even.
b. Highest common factor
c. Least common multiple
d. Multiplication

9. In mathematics, _____ is a property that a binary operation can have. It means that, within an expression containing two or more of the same associative operators in a row, the order that the operations are performed does not matter as long as the sequence of the operands is not changed. That is, rearranging the parentheses in such an expression will not change its value.
   a. Algebraically closed
   b. Associativity
   c. Unital
   d. Idempotence

10. An _____ is a number which is involved in addition. A number being added is considered to be an _____.
    a. A chemical equation
    b. Addend
    c. A Mathematical Theory of Communication
    d. A posteriori

11. The _____ is a rule which states that when you add or multiply numbers, changing the order doesn't change the result.
    a. Commutative law
    b. Semigroupoid
    c. Conditional event algebra
    d. Coimage

12. A _____ is a device for performing mathematical calculations, distinguished from a computer by having a limited problem solving ability and an interface optimized for interactive calculation rather than programming. _____s can be hardware or software, and mechanical or electronic, and are often built into devices such as PDAs or mobile phones.

    Modern electronic _____s are generally small, digital, and usually inexpensive.

    a. Calculator
    b. 1-center problem
    c. 2-3 heap
    d. 120-cell

13. The _____ is the length of the line that bounds an area In the special case where the area is circular, the _____ is known as the circumference.

Chapter 1. WHOLE NUMBERS

  a. Reflection symmetry
  b. Perimeter
  c. Multilateration
  d. Concyclic

14. The traditional names for the parts of the formula c − b = a, are _____ (c) − subtrahend (b) = difference (a). The words _____ and subtrahend are uncommon in modern usage. Instead we say that c and −b are terms, and treat subtraction as addition of the opposite. The answer is still called the difference.
  a. Multiplication
  b. Minuend
  c. Plus and minus signs
  d. Lowest common denominator

15. The quantity that is deducted from the minuend in subtraction is the _____.
  a. Lowest common denominator
  b. The number 0 is even.
  c. Subtrahend
  d. Trailing zeros

16. In mathematics, a _____ is a picture of a straight line in which the integers are shown as specially-marked points evenly spaced on the line. Although this image only shows the integers from -9 to 9, the line includes all real numbers, continuing 'forever' in each direction. It is often used as an aid in teaching simple addition and subtraction, especially involving negative numbers.
  a. Point plotting
  b. Real number
  c. Number line
  d. Number system

17. _____ involves reducing the number of significant digits in a number. The result of _____ is a 'shorter' number having fewer non-zero digits yet similar in magnitude. The result is less precise but easier to use.
  a. Sudan function
  b. Shabakh
  c. Hyper operator
  d. Rounding

Chapter 1. WHOLE NUMBERS

18. A _____ is a software program that facilitates symbolic mathematics. The core functionality of a CAS is manipulation of mathematical expressions in symbolic form.

The symbolic manipulations supported typically include

- simplification to the smallest possible expression or some standard form, including automatic simplification with assumptions and simplification with constraints
- substitution of symbolic, functors or numeric values for expressions
- change of form of expressions: expanding products and powers, partial and full factorization, rewriting as partial fractions, constraint satisfaction, rewriting trigonometric functions as exponentials, etc.
- partial and total differentiation
- symbolic constrained and unconstrained global optimization
- solution of linear and some non-linear equations over various domains
- solution of some differential and difference equations
- taking some limits
- some indefinite and definite integration, including multidimensional integrals
- integral transforms
- arbitrary-precision numeric operations
- Series operations such as expansion, summation and products
- matrix operations including products, inverses, etc.
- display of mathematical expressions in two-dimensional mathematical form, often using typesetting systems similar to TeX
- add-ons for use in applied mathematics such as physics packages for physical computation
- plotting graphs and parametric plots of functions in two and three dimensions, and animating them
- APIs for linking it on an external program such as a database, or using in a programming language to use the _____
- drawing charts and diagrams
- string manipulation such as matching and searching
- statistical computation
- Theorem proving and verification
- graphic production and editing such as CGI and signal processing as image processing
- sound synthesis

Many also include a programming language, allowing users to implement their own algorithms.

Some _____s focus on a specific area of application; these are typically developed in academia and are free.

a. 2-3 heap
b. 120-cell
c. 1-center problem
d. Computer algebra system

Chapter 1. WHOLE NUMBERS

19. In mathematics, an _____ in the sense of ring theory is a subring $\mathcal{O}$ of a ring R that satisfies the conditions

   1. R is a ring which is a finite-dimensional algebra over the rational number field $\mathbb{Q}$
   2. $\mathcal{O}$ spans R over $\mathbb{Q}$, so that $\mathbb{Q}\mathcal{O} = R$, and
   3. $\mathcal{O}$ is a lattice in R.

The third condition can be stated more accurately, in terms of the extension of scalars of R to the real numbers, embedding R in a real vector space. In less formal terms, additively $\mathcal{O}$ should be a free abelian group generated by a basis for R over $\mathbb{Q}$.

The leading example is the case where R is a number field K and $\mathcal{O}$ is its ring of integers. In algebraic number theory there are examples for any K other than the rational field of proper subrings of the ring of integers that are also _____ s.

   a. Algebraic
   b. Efficiency
   c. Annihilator
   d. Order

20. A pair of angles is _____ if their measurements add up to 180 degrees. If the two _____ angles are adjacent their non-shared sides form a straight line. The supplement of 135 would be 45.
   a. Cylinder
   b. Dense
   c. FISH
   d. Supplementary

21. In geometry and trigonometry, an _____ is the figure formed by two rays sharing a common endpoint, called the vertex of the _____. The magnitude of the _____ is the 'amount of rotation' that separates the two rays, and can be measured by considering the length of circular arc swept out when one ray is rotated about the vertex to coincide with the other. Where there is no possibility of confusion, the term '_____' is used interchangeably for both the geometric configuration itself and for its angular magnitude.
   a. A chemical equation
   b. Angle
   c. A Mathematical Theory of Communication
   d. A posteriori

22. In mathematics, an inequality is a statement about the relative size or order of two objects. For example 14 > 10, or 14 is _____ 10. The notation a > b means that a is _____ b and 'a' would be to the right of 'b' on a number line.

Chapter 1. WHOLE NUMBERS

a. Minkowski inequality
b. Cauchy-Schwarz inequality
c. FKG inequality
d. Greater than

23. In mathematics, an _____ is a statement about the relative size or order of two objects, or about whether they are the same or not

- The notation a < b means that a is less than b.
- The notation a > b means that a is greater than b.
- The notation a ≠ b means that a is not equal to b, but does not say that one is bigger than the other or even that they can be compared in size.

In all these cases, a is not equal to b, hence, '_____'.

These relations are known as strict _____

- The notation a ≤ b means that a is less than or equal to b;
- The notation a ≥ b means that a is greater than or equal to b;

An additional use of the notation is to show that one quantity is much greater than another, normally by several orders of magnitude.

- The notation a << b means that a is much less than b.
- The notation a >> b means that a is much greater than b.

If the sense of the _____ is the same for all values of the variables for which its members are defined, then the _____ is called an 'absolute' or 'unconditional' _____. If the sense of an _____ holds only for certain values of the variables involved, but is reversed or destroyed for other values of the variables, it is called a conditional _____.

An _____ may appear unsolvable because it only states whether a number is larger or smaller than another number; but it is possible to apply the same operations for equalities to inequalities. For example, to find x for the _____ 10x > 23 one would divide 23 by 10.

a. A posteriori
b. A Mathematical Theory of Communication
c. A chemical equation
d. Inequality

Chapter 1. WHOLE NUMBERS

24. In computer science an _____ is a data structure consisting of a group of elements that are accessed by indexing. In most programming languages each element has the same data type and the _____ occupies a contiguous area of storage.

Most programming languages have a built-in _____ data type, although what is called an _____ in the language documentation is sometimes really an associative _____.

   a. A posteriori
   b. Array
   c. A Mathematical Theory of Communication
   d. A chemical equation

25. _____ was a German polymath who wrote primarily in Latin and French.

He occupies an equally grand place in both the history of philosophy and the history of mathematics. He invented infinitesimal calculus independently of Newton, and his notation is the one in general use since then.

   a. Michel Rolle
   b. Raymond Merrill Smullyan
   c. Gottfried Wilhelm Leibniz
   d. Harry Hinsley

26. In mathematics, the term _____ has several different important meanings:

   - An _____ is an equality that remains true regardless of the values of any variables that appear within it, to distinguish it from an equality which is true under more particular conditions. For this, the 'triple bar' symbol ≡ is sometimes used.
   - In algebra, an _____ or _____ element of a set S with a binary operation Â· is an element e that, when combined with any element x of S, produces that same x. That is, eÂ·x = xÂ·e = x for all x in S.
     - The _____ function from a set S to itself, often denoted id or id$_S$, s the function such that i = x for all x in S. This function serves as the _____ element in the set of all functions from S to itself with respect to function composition.
     - In linear algebra, the _____ matrix of size n is the n-by-n square matrix with ones on the main diagonal and zeros elsewhere. This matrix serves as the _____ with respect to matrix multiplication.

A common example of the first meaning is the trigonometric _____

$$\sin^2 \theta + \cos^2 \theta = 1$$

Chapter 1. WHOLE NUMBERS

which is true for all real values of θ, as opposed to

$$\cos\theta = 1,$$

which is true only for some values of θ, not all. For example, the latter equation is true when $\theta = 0$, false when $\theta = 2$

The concepts of 'additive _____' and 'multiplicative _____' are central to the Peano axioms. The number 0 is the 'additive _____' for integers, real numbers, and complex numbers. For the real numbers, for all $a \in \mathbb{R}$,

$$0 + a = a,$$

$a + 0 = a$, and

$$0 + 0 = 0.$$

Similarly, The number 1 is the 'multiplicative _____' for integers, real numbers, and complex numbers.

a. Action
b. Identity
c. ARIA
d. Intersection

27. In mathematics, and in particular in abstract algebra, distributivity is a property of binary operations that generalises the _____ law from elementary algebra.
a. General linear group
b. Closure with a twist
c. Permutation
d. Distributive

28. _____ is a quantity expressing the two-dimensional size of a defined part of a surface, typically a region bounded by a closed curve. The term surface _____ refers to the total _____ of the exposed surface of a 3-dimensional solid, such as the sum of the _____s of the exposed sides of a polyhedron. _____ is an important invariant in the differential geometry of surfaces.

a. A posteriori
b. Area
c. A chemical equation
d. A Mathematical Theory of Communication

29. In geometry, a _____ is defined as a quadrilateral where all four of its angles are right angles.
   a. Point group in two dimensions
   b. Polytope
   c. Cantor-Dedekind axiom
   d. Rectangle

30. _____s are payments made by a corporation to its shareholder members. When a corporation earns a profit or surplus, that money can be put to two uses: it can either be re-invested in the business, or it can be paid to the shareholders as a _____. Many corporations retain a portion of their earnings and pay the remainder as a _____.
   a. 1-center problem
   b. 120-cell
   c. GNU Privacy Guard
   d. Dividend

31. In mathematics, a _____ of an integer n is an integer which evenly divides n without leaving a remainder.

For example, 7 is a _____ of 42 because 42/7 = 6. We also say 42 is divisible by 7 or 42 is a multiple of 7 or 7 divides 42 or 7 is a factor of 42 and we usually write 7 | 42.

   a. 1-center problem
   b. 120-cell
   c. Divisor
   d. 2-3 heap

32. In mathematics, a _____ is the end result of a division problem. It can also be expressed as the number of times the divisor divides into the dividend.
   a. Limiting
   b. Notation
   c. Marginal cost
   d. Quotient

Chapter 1. WHOLE NUMBERS

33. In mathematics, a division is called a _____ if the divisor is zero. Such a division can be formally expressed as $\frac{a}{0}$ where a is the dividend. Whether this expression can be assigned a well-defined value depends upon the mathematical setting.

   a. 120-cell
   b. 2-3 heap
   c. Division by Zero
   d. 1-center problem

34. In the mathematical discipline of graph theory, a graph labeling is the assignment of labels, traditionally represented with integers, to the edges or vertices of a graph.

Formally, given a graph G: = with V being the set of vertices and E being the set of edges, a vertex labeling is a function from some subset of the integers to the verticies of the graph. A graph with such function defined is called a vertex-_____.

   a. 2-3 heap
   b. 1-center problem
   c. 120-cell
   d. Labeled graph

35. In mathematics and computer science, _____ (also base-16, hexa or base, of 16. It uses sixteen distinct symbols, most often the symbols 0-9 to represent values zero to nine, and A, B, C, D, E, F (or a through f) to represent values ten to fifteen.

Its primary use is as a human friendly representation of binary coded values, so it is often used in digital electronics and computer engineering.

   a. Factoradic
   b. Tetradecimal
   c. Radix
   d. Hexadecimal

36. Exponentiation is a mathematical operation, written a^n, involving two numbers, the base a and the _____ n. When n is a positive integer, exponentiation corresponds to repeated multiplication:

$$a^n = \underbrace{a \times \cdots \times a}_{n},$$

just as multiplication by a positive integer corresponds to repeated addition:

$$a \times n = \underbrace{a + \cdots + a}_{n}.$$

The _____ is usually shown as a superscript to the right of the base. The exponentiation a^n can be read as: a raised to the n-th power, a raised to the power [of] n or possibly a raised to the _____ [of] n, or more briefly: a to the n-th power or a to the power [of] n, or even more briefly: a to the n.

  a. Exponential tree
  b. Exponent
  c. Exponential sum
  d. Exponentiating by squaring

37. Scientific notation, also sometimes known as standard form or as _____, is a way of writing numbers that accommodates values too large or small to be conveniently written in standard decimal notation. Scientific notation has a number of useful properties and is often favored by scientists, mathematicians and engineers, who work with such numbers.

In scientific notation, numbers are written in the form:

$$a \times 10^b$$

  a. Exponential notation
  b. A Mathematical Theory of Communication
  c. A posteriori
  d. A chemical equation

38. In abstract algebra, a field extension L /K is called _____ if every element of L is _____ over K. Field extensions which are not _____.

For example, the field extension R/Q, that is the field of real numbers as an extension of the field of rational numbers, is transcendental, while the field extensions C/R and Q

  a. Echo
  b. Ideal
  c. Identity
  d. Algebraic

39. In algebra and computer programming, when a number or expression is both preceded and followed by a binary operation, a rule is required for which operation should be applied first; this rule is known as an _____ . From the earliest use of mathematical notation, multiplication took precedence over addition, whichever side of a number it appeared on. Thus 3 + 4 × 5 = 5 × 4 + 3 = 23.
   a. Algebraic K-theory
   b. Isomorphism class
   c. Identity element
   d. Order of operations

40. In mathematics, an _____, or central tendency of a data set refers to a measure of the 'middle' or 'expected' value of the data set. There are many different descriptive statistics that can be chosen as a measurement of the central tendency of the data items.

An _____ is a single value that is meant to typify a list of values.

   a. A Mathematical Theory of Communication
   b. A posteriori
   c. Average
   d. A chemical equation

Chapter 2. INTRODUCTION TO INTEGERS AND ALGEBRAIC EXPRESSIONS

1. The _____ are the set of numbers consisting of the natural numbers including 0 and their negatives. They are numbers that can be written without a fractional or decimal component, and fall within the set {... −2, −1, 0, 1, 2, ...}.
    a. Integers
    b. A posteriori
    c. A Mathematical Theory of Communication
    d. A chemical equation

2. In mathematics, the _____ of a number n is the number that, when added to n, yields zero. The _____ of n is denoted −n. For example, 7 is −7, because 7 + (−7) = 0, and the _____ of −0.3 is 0.3, because −0.3 + 0.3 = 0.
    a. Arity
    b. Algebraic structure
    c. Associativity
    d. Additive inverse

3. A _____ number is a positive integer which has a positive divisor other than one or itself. By definition, every integer greater than one is either a prime number or a _____ number.zero and one are considered to be neither prime nor _____. For example, the integer 14 is a _____ number because it can be factored as 2 × 7.
    a. Discontinuity
    b. Basis
    c. Key server
    d. Composite

4. A _____ is a device for performing mathematical calculations, distinguished from a computer by having a limited problem solving ability and an interface optimized for interactive calculation rather than programming. _____s can be hardware or software, and mechanical or electronic, and are often built into devices such as PDAs or mobile phones.

    Modern electronic _____s are generally small, digital, and usually inexpensive.

    a. 120-cell
    b. 1-center problem
    c. 2-3 heap
    d. Calculator

5. The _____ is a rule which states that when you add or multiply numbers, changing the order doesn't change the result.

Chapter 2. INTRODUCTION TO INTEGERS AND ALGEBRAIC EXPRESSIONS

a. Conditional event algebra
b. Commutative law
c. Semigroupoid
d. Coimage

6. In mathematics, an inequality is a statement about the relative size or order of two objects. For example 14 > 10, or 14 is _____ 10. The notation a > b means that a is _____ b and 'a' would be to the right of 'b' on a number line.
   a. FKG inequality
   b. Greater than
   c. Cauchy-Schwarz inequality
   d. Minkowski inequality

7. In mathematics, a _____ is a picture of a straight line in which the integers are shown as specially-marked points evenly spaced on the line. Although this image only shows the integers from -9 to 9, the line includes all real numbers, continuing 'forever' in each direction. It is often used as an aid in teaching simple addition and subtraction, especially involving negative numbers.
   a. Real number
   b. Number system
   c. Point plotting
   d. Number line

8. In mathematics, an _____ in the sense of ring theory is a subring $\mathcal{O}$ of a ring R that satisfies the conditions

   1. R is a ring which is a finite-dimensional algebra over the rational number field $\mathbb{Q}$
   2. $\mathcal{O}$ spans R over $\mathbb{Q}$, so that $\mathbb{Q}\mathcal{O} = R$, and
   3. $\mathcal{O}$ is a lattice in R.

The third condition can be stated more accurately, in terms of the extension of scalars of R to the real numbers, embedding R in a real vector space. In less formal terms, additively $\mathcal{O}$ should be a free abelian group generated by a basis for R over $\mathbb{Q}$.

The leading example is the case where R is a number field K and $\mathcal{O}$ is its ring of integers. In algebraic number theory there are examples for any K other than the rational field of proper subrings of the ring of integers that are also _____s.

Chapter 2. INTRODUCTION TO INTEGERS AND ALGEBRAIC EXPRESSIONS

a. Annihilator
b. Algebraic
c. Efficiency
d. Order

9. In mathematics, the _____ of a real number is its numerical value without regard to its sign. So, for example, 3 is the _____ of both 3 and −3.

The _____ of a number a is denoted by $|a|$.

Generalizations of the _____ for real numbers occur in a wide variety of mathematical settings.

a. A Mathematical Theory of Communication
b. A chemical equation
c. Area hyperbolic functions
d. Absolute value

10. _____ is the mathematical operation of scaling one number by another. It is one of the four basic operations in elementary arithmetic.

_____ is defined for whole numbers in terms of repeated addition; for example, 4 multiplied by 3 can be calculated by adding 3 copies of 4 together:

$$4 + 4 + 4 = 12.$$

_____ of rational numbers and real numbers is defined by systematic generalization of this basic idea.

a. Highest common factor
b. The number 0 is even.
c. Least common multiple
d. Multiplication

11. In mathematics the concept of a _____ generalizes notions such as 'length', 'area', and 'volume'. Informally, given some base set, a '_____' is any consistent assignment of 'sizes' to the subsets of the base set. Depending on the application, the 'size' of a subset may be interpreted as its physical size, the amount of something that lies within the subset, or the probability that some random process will yield a result within the subset.

Chapter 2. INTRODUCTION TO INTEGERS AND ALGEBRAIC EXPRESSIONS

a. Measure
b. Congruent
c. Cusp
d. Lattice

12. In abstract algebra, a field extension L /K is called _____ if every element of L is _____ over K. Field extensions which are not _____.

For example, the field extension R/Q, that is the field of real numbers as an extension of the field of rational numbers, is transcendental, while the field extensions C/R and Q

a. Ideal
b. Echo
c. Identity
d. Algebraic

13. An _____ is a number which is involved in addition. A number being added is considered to be an _____.
a. A posteriori
b. A chemical equation
c. A Mathematical Theory of Communication
d. Addend

14. In mathematics the _____ of a set which is equipped with the operation of addition is an element which, when added to any element x in the set, yields x. One of the most familiar additive identities is the number 0 from elementary mathematics, but additive identities occur in other mathematical structures where addition is defined, such as in groups and rings.

- The _____ familiar from elementary mathematics is zero, denoted 0. For example,

  $5 + 0 = 5 = 0 + 5$.

- In the natural numbers N and all of its supersets, the _____ is 0. Thus for any one of these numbers n,

  $n + 0 = n = 0 + n$.

Let N be a set which is closed under the operation of addition, denoted +. An _____ for N is any element e such that for any element n in N,

$e + n = n = n + e$.

Chapter 2. INTRODUCTION TO INTEGERS AND ALGEBRAIC EXPRESSIONS

a. Unique factorization domain
b. Unit ring
c. Algebraically independent
d. Additive identity

15. In mathematics, the term _____ has several different important meanings:

   - An _____ is an equality that remains true regardless of the values of any variables that appear within it, to distinguish it from an equality which is true under more particular conditions. For this, the 'triple bar' symbol ≡ is sometimes used.
   - In algebra, an _____ or _____ element of a set S with a binary operation Â· is an element e that, when combined with any element x of S, produces that same x. That is, eÂ·x = xÂ·e = x for all x in S.
     - The _____ function from a set S to itself, often denoted id or id_S, s the function such that i = x for all x in S. This function serves as the _____ element in the set of all functions from S to itself with respect to function composition.
     - In linear algebra, the _____ matrix of size n is the n-by-n square matrix with ones on the main diagonal and zeros elsewhere. This matrix serves as the _____ with respect to matrix multiplication.

A common example of the first meaning is the trigonometric _____

$$\sin^2 \theta + \cos^2 \theta = 1$$

which is true for all real values of θ, as opposed to

$$\cos \theta = 1,$$

which is true only for some values of θ, not all. For example, the latter equation is true when $\theta = 0$, false when $\theta = 2$

The concepts of 'additive _____' and 'multiplicative _____' are central to the Peano axioms. The number 0 is the 'additive _____' for integers, real numbers, and complex numbers. For the real numbers, for all $a \in \mathbb{R}$,

$$0 + a = a,$$

$$a + 0 = a, \text{ and}$$

$$0 + 0 = 0.$$

Similarly, The number 1 is the 'multiplicative _____' for integers, real numbers, and complex numbers.

Chapter 2. INTRODUCTION TO INTEGERS AND ALGEBRAIC EXPRESSIONS

a. ARIA
b. Action
c. Intersection
d. Identity

16. In mathematics, _____ is a property that a binary operation can have. It means that, within an expression containing two or more of the same associative operators in a row, the order that the operations are performed does not matter as long as the sequence of the operands is not changed. That is, rearranging the parentheses in such an expression will not change its value.
    a. Unital
    b. Associativity
    c. Idempotence
    d. Algebraically closed

17. In mathematics, a _____ is the end result of a division problem. It can also be expressed as the number of times the divisor divides into the dividend.
    a. Marginal cost
    b. Limiting
    c. Notation
    d. Quotient

18. In mathematics, a division is called a _____ if the divisor is zero. Such a division can be formally expressed as $\frac{a}{0}$ where a is the dividend. Whether this expression can be assigned a well-defined value depends upon the mathematical setting.
    a. 1-center problem
    b. 2-3 heap
    c. 120-cell
    d. Division by Zero

19. In algebra and computer programming, when a number or expression is both preceded and followed by a binary operation, a rule is required for which operation should be applied first; this rule is known as an _____ . From the earliest use of mathematical notation, multiplication took precedence over addition, whichever side of a number it appeared on. Thus 3 + 4 × 5 = 5 × 4 + 3 = 23.

Chapter 2. INTRODUCTION TO INTEGERS AND ALGEBRAIC EXPRESSIONS

a. Order of operations
b. Algebraic K-theory
c. Isomorphism class
d. Identity element

20. In mathematics, and in particular in abstract algebra, distributivity is a property of binary operations that generalises the _____ law from elementary algebra.

a. Closure with a twist
b. Distributive
c. Permutation
d. General linear group

21. In the study of metric spaces in mathematics, there are various notions of two metrics on the same underlying space being 'the same', or _____.

In the following, M will denote a non-empty set and d_1 and d_2 will denote two metrics on M.

The two metrics d_1 and d_2 are said to be topologically _____ if they generate the same topology on M.

a. A posteriori
b. A chemical equation
c. A Mathematical Theory of Communication
d. Equivalent

22. In linear algebra, two n-by-n matrices A and B over the field K are called _____ if there exists an invertible n-by-n matrix P over K such that

$$P^{-1}AP = B.$$

One of the meanings of the term similarity transformation is such a transformation of a matrix A into a matrix B.

Similarity is an equivalence relation on the space of square matrices.

Chapter 2. INTRODUCTION TO INTEGERS AND ALGEBRAIC EXPRESSIONS

_____ matrices share many properties:

- rank
- determinant
- trace
- eigenvalues
- characteristic polynomial
- minimal polynomial
- elementary divisors

There are two reasons for these facts:

- two _____ matrices can be thought of as describing the same linear map, but with respect to different bases
- the map $X \mapsto P^{-1}XP$ is an automorphism of the associative algebra of all n-by-n matrices, as the one-object case of the above category of all matrices.

Because of this, for a given matrix A, one is interested in finding a simple 'normal form' B which is _____ to A -- the study of A then reduces to the study of the simpler matrix B.

a. Blinding
b. Dense
c. Coherence
d. Similar

23. The _____ is the length of the line that bounds an area In the special case where the area is circular, the _____ is known as the circumference.
a. Reflection symmetry
b. Concyclic
c. Multilateration
d. Perimeter

24. In geometry a _____ is traditionally a plane figure that is bounded by a closed path or circuit, composed of a finite sequence of straight line segments. These segments are called its edges or sides, and the points where two edges meet are the _____ 's vertices or corners. The interior of the _____ is sometimes called its body.

a. Polygon
b. Polygonal curve
c. Parallelogon
d. Regular polygon

25. In geometry and trigonometry, an _____ is the figure formed by two rays sharing a common endpoint, called the vertex of the _____. The magnitude of the _____ is the 'amount of rotation' that separates the two rays, and can be measured by considering the length of circular arc swept out when one ray is rotated about the vertex to coincide with the other. Where there is no possibility of confusion, the term '_____' is used interchangeably for both the geometric configuration itself and for its angular magnitude.
   a. A chemical equation
   b. A Mathematical Theory of Communication
   c. A posteriori
   d. Angle

26. In geometry, a _____ is defined as a quadrilateral where all four of its angles are right angles.
   a. Polytope
   b. Point group in two dimensions
   c. Rectangle
   d. Cantor-Dedekind axiom

27. In geometry and trigonometry, a _____ is defined as an angle between two straight intersecting lines of ninety degrees, or one-quarter of a circle.
   a. Trigonometry
   b. Trigonometric functions
   c. Sine integral
   d. Right angle

Chapter 3. FRACTION NOTATION: MULTIPLICATION AND DIVISION

1. In mathematics, a _____ can mean either an element of the set {1, 2, 3, ...} or an element of the set {0, 1, 2, 3, ...}. The latter is especially preferred in mathematical logic, set theory, and computer science.

    _____s have two main purposes: they can be used for counting, and they can be used for ordering.

    a. Strong partition cardinal
    b. Suslin cardinal
    c. Cardinal numbers
    d. Natural number

2. A _____ is a device for performing mathematical calculations, distinguished from a computer by having a limited problem solving ability and an interface optimized for interactive calculation rather than programming. _____s can be hardware or software, and mechanical or electronic, and are often built into devices such as PDAs or mobile phones.

    Modern electronic _____s are generally small, digital, and usually inexpensive.

    a. 1-center problem
    b. 120-cell
    c. 2-3 heap
    d. Calculator

3. A _____ number is a positive integer which has a positive divisor other than one or itself. By definition, every integer greater than one is either a prime number or a _____ number. zero and one are considered to be neither prime nor _____. For example, the integer 14 is a _____ number because it can be factored as 2 × 7.
    a. Discontinuity
    b. Basis
    c. Key server
    d. Composite

4. In mathematics the concept of a _____ generalizes notions such as 'length', 'area', and 'volume'. Informally, given some base set, a '_____' is any consistent assignment of 'sizes' to the subsets of the base set. Depending on the application, the 'size' of a subset may be interpreted as its physical size, the amount of something that lies within the subset, or the probability that some random process will yield a result within the subset.
    a. Cusp
    b. Congruent
    c. Lattice
    d. Measure

Chapter 3. FRACTION NOTATION: MULTIPLICATION AND DIVISION

5. A _____ is a positive integer which has a positive divisor other than one or itself. In other words, if 0 < n is an integer and there are integers 1 < a, b < n such that n = a × b then n is composite. By definition, every integer greater than one is either a prime number or a _____.

 a. Prime Pages
 b. Megaprime
 c. Composite number
 d. Ruth-Aaron pair

6. In mathematics, a _____ is a natural number which has exactly two distinct natural number divisors: 1 and itself. An infinitude of _____s exists, as demonstrated by Euclid around 300 BC. The first twenty-five _____s are:

 2, 3, 5, 7, 11, 13, 17, 19, 23, 29, 31, 37, 41, 43, 47, 53, 59, 61, 67, 71, 73, 79, 83, 89, 97.

 a. Pronic number
 b. Perrin number
 c. Highly composite number
 d. Prime number

7. In number theory, the _____ states that every natural number greater than 1 can be written as a unique product of prime numbers. For instance,

$$6936 = 2^3 \times 3 \times 17^2,$$

$$1200 = 2^4 \times 3 \times 5^2.$$

There are no other possible factorizations of 6936 or 1200 into non-negative prime numbers. The above representation collapses repeated prime factors into powers for easier identification.

 a. Feit–Thompson theorem
 b. Dedekind sums
 c. Cyclic number
 d. Fundamental Theorem of Arithmetic

8. In mathematics, a _____ is a statement that can be proved on the basis of explicitly stated or previously agreed assumptions.

Chapter 3. FRACTION NOTATION: MULTIPLICATION AND DIVISION

a. Logical value
b. Boolean function
c. Theorem
d. Disjunction introduction

9. In set theory, a _____ is a partially ordered set such that for each t ∈ T, the set {s ∈ T : s < t} is well-ordered by the relation <. For each t ∈ T, the order type of {s ∈ T : s < t} is called the height of t. The height of T itself is the least ordinal greater than the height of each element of T.
   a. Transitive reduction
   b. Set-theoretic topology
   c. Definable numbers
   d. Tree

10. In number theory, a _____ of a positive integer n is a way of writing n as a sum of positive integers. Two sums which only differ in the order of their summands are considered to be the same _____; if order matters then the sum becomes a composition. A summand in a _____ is also called a part.
    a. Congruent
    b. Derivative algebra
    c. Partition
    d. Distribution

11. A _____ is a simple shape of Euclidean geometry consisting of those points in a plane which are at a constant distance, called the radius, from a fixed point, called the center. A _____ with center A is sometimes denoted by the symbol A.

    A chord of a _____ is a line segment whose two endpoints lie on the _____.

    a. Malfatti circles
    b. Circumcircle
    c. Circle
    d. Circular segment

12. In graph theory, a _____ is a graph whose vertices can be associated with chords of a circle such that two vertices are adjacent if and only if the corresponding chords in the circle intersect.

    Spinrad (1994) gives an $O(n^2)$-time recognition algorithm for _____s that also computes a circle model of the input graph if it is a _____.

A number of other problems that are NP-complete on general graphs have polynomial time algorithms when restricted to _____s.

a. Circle graph
b. Sparse graph
c. Planar graph
d. Vertex-transitive graph

13. A _____ is a circular chart divided into sectors, illustrating relative magnitudes or frequences or percents. In a _____, the arc length of each sector, is proportional to the quantity it represents. Together, the sectors create a full disk.
a. Pie chart
b. 2-3 heap
c. 120-cell
d. 1-center problem

14. The _____ are the set of numbers consisting of the natural numbers including 0 and their negatives. They are numbers that can be written without a fractional or decimal component, and fall within the set {... −2, −1, 0, 1, 2, ...}.
a. A Mathematical Theory of Communication
b. A posteriori
c. A chemical equation
d. Integers

15. In mathematics, a division is called a _____ if the divisor is zero. Such a division can be formally expressed as $\frac{a}{0}$ where a is the dividend. Whether this expression can be assigned a well-defined value depends upon the mathematical setting.
a. 1-center problem
b. 2-3 heap
c. 120-cell
d. Division by Zero

16. _____ is the mathematical operation of scaling one number by another. It is one of the four basic operations in elementary arithmetic.

_____ is defined for whole numbers in terms of repeated addition; for example, 4 multiplied by 3 can be calculated by adding 3 copies of 4 together:

$$4 + 4 + 4 = 12.$$

_____ of rational numbers and real numbers is defined by systematic generalization of this basic idea.

   a. Multiplication
   b. Least common multiple
   c. Highest common factor
   d. The number 0 is even.

17. In mathematics, _____ is a property that a binary operation can have. It means that, within an expression containing two or more of the same associative operators in a row, the order that the operations are performed does not matter as long as the sequence of the operands is not changed. That is, rearranging the parentheses in such an expression will not change its value.
   a. Algebraically closed
   b. Idempotence
   c. Unital
   d. Associativity

18. In geometry, a _____ is defined as a quadrilateral where all four of its angles are right angles.
   a. Rectangle
   b. Cantor-Dedekind axiom
   c. Point group in two dimensions
   d. Polytope

19. _____ is a quantity expressing the two-dimensional size of a defined part of a surface, typically a region bounded by a closed curve. The term surface _____ refers to the total _____ of the exposed surface of a 3-dimensional solid, such as the sum of the _____s of the exposed sides of a polyhedron. _____ is an important invariant in the differential geometry of surfaces.
   a. A posteriori
   b. A Mathematical Theory of Communication
   c. A chemical equation
   d. Area

Chapter 3. FRACTION NOTATION: MULTIPLICATION AND DIVISION

20. In the study of metric spaces in mathematics, there are various notions of two metrics on the same underlying space being 'the same', or _____.

In the following, M will denote a non-empty set and d_1 and d_2 will denote two metrics on M.

The two metrics d_1 and d_2 are said to be topologically _____ if they generate the same topology on M.

a. A Mathematical Theory of Communication
b. A chemical equation
c. A posteriori
d. Equivalent

21. In mathematics, the term _____ has several different important meanings:

- An _____ is an equality that remains true regardless of the values of any variables that appear within it, to distinguish it from an equality which is true under more particular conditions. For this, the 'triple bar' symbol ≡ is sometimes used.
- In algebra, an _____ or _____ element of a set S with a binary operation Â· is an element e that, when combined with any element x of S, produces that same x. That is, eÂ·x = xÂ·e = x for all x in S.
  - The _____ function from a set S to itself, often denoted id or id_S, s the function such that i = x for all x in S. This function serves as the _____ element in the set of all functions from S to itself with respect to function composition.
  - In linear algebra, the _____ matrix of size n is the n-by-n square matrix with ones on the main diagonal and zeros elsewhere. This matrix serves as the _____ with respect to matrix multiplication.

A common example of the first meaning is the trigonometric _____

$$\sin^2 \theta + \cos^2 \theta = 1$$

which is true for all real values of θ, as opposed to

$$\cos \theta = 1,$$

which is true only for some values of θ, not all. For example, the latter equation is true when $\theta = 0$, false when $\theta = 2$

Chapter 3. FRACTION NOTATION: MULTIPLICATION AND DIVISION

The concepts of 'additive _____' and 'multiplicative _____' are central to the Peano axioms. The number 0 is the 'additive _____' for integers, real numbers, and complex numbers. For the real numbers, for all $a \in \mathbb{R}$,

$$0 + a = a,$$

$$a + 0 = a, \text{ and}$$

$$0 + 0 = 0.$$

Similarly, The number 1 is the 'multiplicative _____' for integers, real numbers, and complex numbers.

a. Intersection
b. ARIA
c. Action
d. Identity

22. In mathematics, the _____ or least common denominator is the least common multiple of the denominators of a set of vulgar fractions. It is the smallest positive integer that is a multiple of the denominators. For instance, the _____ of

$$\left\{ \frac{5}{12}, \frac{11}{18} \right\}$$

is 36 because the least common multiple of 12 and 18 is 36.

a. Highest common factor
b. Subtrahend
c. The number 0 is even.
d. Lowest common denominator

23. A _____ is one of the basic shapes of geometry: a polygon with three corners or vertices and three sides or edges which are line segments. A _____ with vertices A, B, and C is denoted ABC.

In Euclidean geometry any three non-collinear points determine a unique _____ and a unique plane.

Chapter 3. FRACTION NOTATION: MULTIPLICATION AND DIVISION

a. 1-center problem
b. Fuhrmann circle
c. Kepler triangle
d. Triangle

24. In mathematics, the _____ of a number n is the number that, when added to n, yields zero. The _____ of n is denoted −n. For example, 7 is −7, because 7 + (−7) = 0, and the _____ of −0.3 is 0.3, because −0.3 + 0.3 = 0.

a. Associativity
b. Algebraic structure
c. Additive inverse
d. Arity

25. In mathematics, a _____ for a number x, denoted by $1/x$ or x^{-1}, is a number which when multiplied by x yields the multiplicative identity, 1. The _____ of x is also called the reciprocal of x. The _____ of a fraction p/q is q/p.

a. Hyperbolic function
b. Golden function
c. Double exponential
d. Multiplicative inverse

26. In mathematics, the multiplicative inverse of a number x, denoted 1/x or x^{-1}, is the number which, when multiplied by x, yields 1. The multiplicative inverse of x is also called the _____ of x.

a. 120-cell
b. 2-3 heap
c. 1-center problem
d. Reciprocal

27. In mathematics, a _____ is a constant multiplicative factor of a certain object. For example, in the expression $9x^2$, the _____ of x^2 is 9.

The object can be such things as a variable, a vector, a function, etc.

a. Stability radius
b. Multivariate division algorithm
c. Fibonacci polynomials
d. Coefficient

28. A _____ is a word, phrase, number or other sequence of units that can be read the same way in either direction. Composing literature in _____s is an example of constrained writing. The word '_____' was coined from Greek roots palin and dromos by English writer Ben Jonson in the 1600s.
   a. Palindrome
   b. Metalanguage
   c. 1-center problem
   d. 120-cell

Chapter 4. FRACTION NOTATION: ADDITION AND SUBTRACTION

1. In arithmetic and number theory, the _____ or lowest common multiple or smallest common multiple of two integers a and b is the smallest positive integer that is a multiple of both a and b. Since it is a multiple, it can be divided by a and b without a remainder. If either a or b is 0, so that there is no such positive integer, then lc is defined to be zero.

    a. Plus and minus signs
    b. Plus-minus sign
    c. Lowest common denominator
    d. Least common multiple

2. In mathematics, a _____ can mean either an element of the set {1, 2, 3, ...} or an element of the set {0, 1, 2, 3, ...}. The latter is especially preferred in mathematical logic, set theory, and computer science.

    _____s have two main purposes: they can be used for counting, and they can be used for ordering.

    a. Strong partition cardinal
    b. Cardinal numbers
    c. Suslin cardinal
    d. Natural number

3. In mathematics, a _____ is a natural number which has exactly two distinct natural number divisors: 1 and itself. An infinitude of _____s exists, as demonstrated by Euclid around 300 BC. The first twenty-five _____s are:

    2, 3, 5, 7, 11, 13, 17, 19, 23, 29, 31, 37, 41, 43, 47, 53, 59, 61, 67, 71, 73, 79, 83, 89, 97.

    a. Prime number
    b. Highly composite number
    c. Pronic number
    d. Perrin number

4. Scientific notation, also sometimes known as standard form or as _____, is a way of writing numbers that accommodates values too large or small to be conveniently written in standard decimal notation. Scientific notation has a number of useful properties and is often favored by scientists, mathematicians and engineers, who work with such numbers.

    In scientific notation, numbers are written in the form:

    $$a \times 10^b$$

Chapter 4. FRACTION NOTATION: ADDITION AND SUBTRACTION

a. A posteriori
b. A Mathematical Theory of Communication
c. Exponential notation
d. A chemical equation

5. An _____ is a number which is involved in addition. A number being added is considered to be an _____.

a. A chemical equation
b. A Mathematical Theory of Communication
c. A posteriori
d. Addend

6. In mathematics, the _____ or least common denominator is the least common multiple of the denominators of a set of vulgar fractions. It is the smallest positive integer that is a multiple of the denominators. For instance, the _____ of

$$\left\{\frac{5}{12}, \frac{11}{18}\right\}$$

is 36 because the least common multiple of 12 and 18 is 36.

a. Subtrahend
b. Highest common factor
c. The number 0 is even.
d. Lowest common denominator

7. _____ is the mathematical operation of scaling one number by another. It is one of the four basic operations in elementary arithmetic.

_____ is defined for whole numbers in terms of repeated addition; for example, 4 multiplied by 3 can be calculated by adding 3 copies of 4 together:

$$4 + 4 + 4 = 12.$$

_____ of rational numbers and real numbers is defined by systematic generalization of this basic idea.

34 *Chapter 4. FRACTION NOTATION: ADDITION AND SUBTRACTION*

   a. The number 0 is even.
   b. Least common multiple
   c. Highest common factor
   d. Multiplication

8. In mathematics, _____ is a property that a binary operation can have. It means that, within an expression containing two or more of the same associative operators in a row, the order that the operations are performed does not matter as long as the sequence of the operands is not changed. That is, rearranging the parentheses in such an expression will not change its value.
   a. Idempotence
   b. Algebraically closed
   c. Unital
   d. Associativity

9. The _____ is a rule which states that when you add or multiply numbers, changing the order doesn't change the result.
   a. Semigroupoid
   b. Coimage
   c. Conditional event algebra
   d. Commutative law

10. In mathematics, an _____ in the sense of ring theory is a subring $\mathcal{O}$ of a ring R that satisfies the conditions

   1. R is a ring which is a finite-dimensional algebra over the rational number field $\mathbb{Q}$
   2. $\mathcal{O}$ spans R over $\mathbb{Q}$, so that $\mathbb{Q}\mathcal{O} = R$, and
   3. $\mathcal{O}$ is a lattice in R.

The third condition can be stated more accurately, in terms of the extension of scalars of R to the real numbers, embedding R in a real vector space. In less formal terms, additively $\mathcal{O}$ should be a free abelian group generated by a basis for R over $\mathbb{Q}$.

The leading example is the case where R is a number field K and $\mathcal{O}$ is its ring of integers. In algebraic number theory there are examples for any K other than the rational field of proper subrings of the ring of integers that are also _____s.

a. Algebraic
b. Annihilator
c. Order
d. Efficiency

11. A _____ is a device for performing mathematical calculations, distinguished from a computer by having a limited problem solving ability and an interface optimized for interactive calculation rather than programming. _____s can be hardware or software, and mechanical or electronic, and are often built into devices such as PDAs or mobile phones.

Modern electronic _____s are generally small, digital, and usually inexpensive.

a. 120-cell
b. 1-center problem
c. 2-3 heap
d. Calculator

12. _____ is a general term for any type of information processing. This includes phenomena ranging from human thinking to calculations with a more narrow meaning. _____ is a process following a well-defined model that is understood and can be expressed in an algorithm, protocol, network topology, etc.

a. Computation
b. 120-cell
c. 2-3 heap
d. 1-center problem

13. In mathematics the concept of a _____ generalizes notions such as 'length', 'area', and 'volume'. Informally, given some base set, a '_____' is any consistent assignment of 'sizes' to the subsets of the base set. Depending on the application, the 'size' of a subset may be interpreted as its physical size, the amount of something that lies within the subset, or the probability that some random process will yield a result within the subset.

a. Congruent
b. Cusp
c. Lattice
d. Measure

14. In mathematics, an _____, or central tendency of a data set refers to a measure of the 'middle' or 'expected' value of the data set. There are many different descriptive statistics that can be chosen as a measurement of the central tendency of the data items.

An _____ is a single value that is meant to typify a list of values.

a. A chemical equation
b. A posteriori
c. A Mathematical Theory of Communication
d. Average

15. In mathematics, a _____ is the end result of a division problem. It can also be expressed as the number of times the divisor divides into the dividend.
   a. Quotient
   b. Marginal cost
   c. Notation
   d. Limiting

16. In abstract algebra, a field extension L /K is called _____ if every element of L is _____ over K. Field extensions which are not _____.

For example, the field extension R/Q, that is the field of real numbers as an extension of the field of rational numbers, is transcendental, while the field extensions C/R and Q

   a. Identity
   b. Echo
   c. Ideal
   d. Algebraic

Chapter 5. DECIMAL NOTATION

1. In a positional numeral system, the decimal separator is a symbol used to mark the boundary between the integral and the fractional parts of a decimal numeral. When used in context of Arabic numerals, terms implying the symbol used are _____ and decimal comma.

The decimal separator is mathematically a radix point.

   a. Hexadecimal
   b. Tetradecimal
   c. Fibonacci coding
   d. Decimal point

2. In mathematics, a _____ is a number which can be expressed as a ratio of two integers. Non-integer _____s are usually written as the vulgar fraction $\frac{a}{b}$, where b is not zero. a is called the numerator, and b the denominator.
   a. Pre-algebra
   b. Minkowski distance
   c. Tally marks
   d. Rational number

3. A _____ number is a positive integer which has a positive divisor other than one or itself. By definition, every integer greater than one is either a prime number or a _____ number.zero and one are considered to be neither prime nor _____. For example, the integer 14 is a _____ number because it can be factored as 2 × 7.
   a. Discontinuity
   b. Basis
   c. Key server
   d. Composite

4. _____ is a numeral system in which each position is related to the next by a constant multiplier, a common ratio, called the base or radix of that numeral system.
   a. Cyrillic numerals
   b. NegaFibonacci coding
   c. Negative base
   d. Place value

5. In mathematics the concept of a _____ generalizes notions such as 'length', 'area', and 'volume'. Informally, given some base set, a '_____' is any consistent assignment of 'sizes' to the subsets of the base set. Depending on the application, the 'size' of a subset may be interpreted as its physical size, the amount of something that lies within the subset, or the probability that some random process will yield a result within the subset.

a. Congruent
b. Measure
c. Cusp
d. Lattice

6. The _____ is a rule which states that when you add or multiply numbers, changing the order doesn't change the result.
   a. Semigroupoid
   b. Commutative law
   c. Conditional event algebra
   d. Coimage

7. In mathematics, an _____ in the sense of ring theory is a subring $\mathcal{O}$ of a ring R that satisfies the conditions

   1. R is a ring which is a finite-dimensional algebra over the rational number field $\mathbb{Q}$
   2. $\mathcal{O}$ spans R over $\mathbb{Q}$, so that $\mathbb{Q}\mathcal{O} = R$, and
   3. $\mathcal{O}$ is a lattice in R.

The third condition can be stated more accurately, in terms of the extension of scalars of R to the real numbers, embedding R in a real vector space. In less formal terms, additively $\mathcal{O}$ should be a free abelian group generated by a basis for R over $\mathbb{Q}$.

The leading example is the case where R is a number field K and $\mathcal{O}$ is its ring of integers. In algebraic number theory there are examples for any K other than the rational field of proper subrings of the ring of integers that are also _____ s.

   a. Algebraic
   b. Efficiency
   c. Annihilator
   d. Order

8. _____ involves reducing the number of significant digits in a number. The result of _____ is a 'shorter' number having fewer non-zero digits yet similar in magnitude. The result is less precise but easier to use.
   a. Hyper operator
   b. Shabakh
   c. Sudan function
   d. Rounding

Chapter 5. DECIMAL NOTATION

9. An _____ is a number which is involved in addition. A number being added is considered to be an _____.
   a. Addend
   b. A Mathematical Theory of Communication
   c. A posteriori
   d. A chemical equation

10. _____ is the mathematical operation of scaling one number by another. It is one of the four basic operations in elementary arithmetic.

    _____ is defined for whole numbers in terms of repeated addition; for example, 4 multiplied by 3 can be calculated by adding 3 copies of 4 together:

    $$4 + 4 + 4 = 12.$$

    _____ of rational numbers and real numbers is defined by systematic generalization of this basic idea.

    a. Highest common factor
    b. Least common multiple
    c. The number 0 is even.
    d. Multiplication

11. In mathematics, _____ is a property that a binary operation can have. It means that, within an expression containing two or more of the same associative operators in a row, the order that the operations are performed does not matter as long as the sequence of the operands is not changed. That is, rearranging the parentheses in such an expression will not change its value.
    a. Unital
    b. Algebraically closed
    c. Associativity
    d. Idempotence

12. A _____ is a device for performing mathematical calculations, distinguished from a computer by having a limited problem solving ability and an interface optimized for interactive calculation rather than programming. _____s can be hardware or software, and mechanical or electronic, and are often built into devices such as PDAs or mobile phones.

    Modern electronic _____s are generally small, digital, and usually inexpensive.

Chapter 5. DECIMAL NOTATION

   a. 2-3 heap
   b. 120-cell
   c. Calculator
   d. 1-center problem

13. In mathematics and physics, there are a _____ number of topics named in honor of Leonhard Euler. As well, many of these topics include their own unique function, equation, formula, identity, number, or other mathematical entity. Unfortunately however, many of these entities have been given simple names like Euler's function, Euler's equation, and Euler's formula, which are further confused by variations of the 'Euler'-prefix Overall though, Euler's work touched upon so many fields that he is often the earliest written reference on a given matter.
   a. List of integrals of logarithmic functions
   b. List of mathematical knots and links
   c. Large
   d. List of trigonometry topics

14. In abstract algebra, a field extension L /K is called _____ if every element of L is _____ over K. Field extensions which are not _____.

For example, the field extension R/Q, that is the field of real numbers as an extension of the field of rational numbers, is transcendental, while the field extensions C/R and Q

   a. Ideal
   b. Echo
   c. Identity
   d. Algebraic

15. In mathematics, a _____ can mean either an element of the set {1, 2, 3, ...} (i.e the positive integers) or an element of the set {0, 1, 2, 3, ...} (i.e. the non-negative integers).
   a. FISH
   b. Bounded
   c. Degrees of freedom
   d. Whole number

16. In algebra and computer programming, when a number or expression is both preceded and followed by a binary operation, a rule is required for which operation should be applied first; this rule is known as an _____ . From the earliest use of mathematical notation, multiplication took precedence over addition, whichever side of a number it appeared on. Thus 3 + 4 × 5 = 5 × 4 + 3 = 23.

a. Isomorphism class
b. Algebraic K-theory
c. Identity element
d. Order of operations

17. A _____ is a deliberate process for transforming one or more inputs into one or more results, with variable change.

The term is used in a variety of senses, from the very definite arithmetical using an algorithm to the vague heuristics of calculating a strategy in a competition or calculating the chance of a successful relationship between two people.

Multiplying 7 by 8 is a simple algorithmic _____.

a. Mathematics Subject Classification
b. Mathematical maturity
c. Mathematical object
d. Calculation

18. In mathematics, a _____ is the end result of a division problem. It can also be expressed as the number of times the divisor divides into the dividend.
a. Notation
b. Marginal cost
c. Quotient
d. Limiting

19. A _____ is a simple shape of Euclidean geometry consisting of those points in a plane which are at a constant distance, called the radius, from a fixed point, called the center. A _____ with center A is sometimes denoted by the symbol A.

A chord of a _____ is a line segment whose two endpoints lie on the _____.

a. Malfatti circles
b. Circular segment
c. Circumcircle
d. Circle

Chapter 5. DECIMAL NOTATION

20. In classical geometry, a _____ of a circle or sphere is any line segment from its center to its boundary. By extension, the _____ of a circle or sphere is the length of any such segment. The _____ is half the diameter. In science and engineering the term _____ of curvature is commonly used as a synonym for _____.

   a. Non-Euclidean geometry
   b. Radius
   c. Duoprism
   d. Birational geometry

21. _____ is a quantity expressing the two-dimensional size of a defined part of a surface, typically a region bounded by a closed curve. The term surface _____ refers to the total _____ of the exposed surface of a 3-dimensional solid, such as the sum of the _____s of the exposed sides of a polyhedron. _____ is an important invariant in the differential geometry of surfaces.

   a. A posteriori
   b. A Mathematical Theory of Communication
   c. A chemical equation
   d. Area

22. _____ is a term used in accounting, economics and finance to spread the cost of an asset over the span of several years.

   In simple words we can say that _____ is the reduction in the value of an asset due to usage, passage of time, wear and tear, technological outdating or obsolescence, depletion or other such factors.

   In accounting, _____ is a term used to describe any method of attributing the historical or purchase cost of an asset across its useful life, roughly corresponding to normal wear and tear.

   a. 120-cell
   b. Depreciation
   c. 1-center problem
   d. Gross sales

Chapter 6. INTRODUCTION TO GRAPHING AND STATISTICS

1. In mathematics the concept of a _____ generalizes notions such as 'length', 'area', and 'volume'. Informally, given some base set, a '_____' is any consistent assignment of 'sizes' to the subsets of the base set. Depending on the application, the 'size' of a subset may be interpreted as its physical size, the amount of something that lies within the subset, or the probability that some random process will yield a result within the subset.
   a. Lattice
   b. Cusp
   c. Congruent
   d. Measure

2. _____ or pictograph is a symbol representing a concept, object, activity, place or event by illustration. Pictography is a form of writing in which ideas are transmitted through drawing. It is a basis of cuneiform and, to some extent, hieroglyphic writing, which uses drawings also as phonetic letters or determinative rhymes.
   a. Sparkline
   b. Pictographs
   c. Treemapping
   d. Pictogram

3. _____ are symbols representing a concept, object, activity, place or event by illustration.
   a. Treemapping
   b. Pictogram
   c. Sparkline
   d. Pictographs

4. A bar chart or _____ is a chart with rectangular bars with lengths proportional to the values that they represent. Bar charts are used for comparing two or more values. The bars can be horizontally or vertically oriented.
   a. 120-cell
   b. 2-3 heap
   c. Bar graph
   d. 1-center problem

5. In a graph theory, the _____ L

One of the earliest and most important theorems about _____s is due to Hassler Whitney, who proved that with one exceptional case the structure of G can be recovered completely from its _____.

Chapter 6. INTRODUCTION TO GRAPHING AND STATISTICS

   a. Bivariegated graph
   b. Sparse graph
   c. Vertex-transitive graph
   d. Line graph

6. In quantum field theory and statistical mechanics in the thermodynamic limit, a system with a global symmetry can have more than one phase. For parameters where the symmetry is spontaneously broken, the system is said to be _____. When the global symmetry is unbroken the system is disordered.
   a. Isoenthalpic-isobaric ensemble
   b. Ursell function
   c. Einstein relation
   d. Ordered

7. In mathematics, an _____ is a collection of objects having two coordinates (or entries or projections), such that one can always uniquely determine the object, which is the first coordinate (or first entry or left projection) of the pair as well as the second coordinate (or second entry or right projection.) If the first coordinate is a and the second is b, the usual notation for an _____ is (a, b.) The pair is 'ordered' in that (a, b) differs from (b, a) unless a = b.
   a. Ordered pair
   b. A chemical equation
   c. A Mathematical Theory of Communication
   d. A posteriori

8. In mathematics, the _____ of a Euclidean space is a special point, usually denoted by the letter O, used as a fixed point of reference for the geometry of the surrounding space. In a Cartesian coordinate system, the _____ is the point where the axes of the system intersect. In Euclidean geometry, the _____ may be chosen freely as any convenient point of reference.
   a. Origin
   b. Interval
   c. Autonomous system
   d. OMAC

9. In mathematics, a _____ is, informally, an infinitely vast and infinitely thin sheet. _____s may be thought of as objects in some higher dimensional space, or they may be considered without any outside space, as in the setting of Euclidean geometry

Chapter 6. INTRODUCTION TO GRAPHING AND STATISTICS

a. Group
b. Blocking
c. Plane
d. Bandwidth

10. The x-axis is the horizontal axis of a two-dimensional plot in the _____, that is typically pointed to the right. Also known as a right-handed coordinate system.

a. 120-cell
b. 1-center problem
c. 2-3 heap
d. Cartesian coordinate system

11. A _____ is an algebraic equation in which each term is either a constant or the product of a constant and a single variable. _____s can have one, two, three or more variables.

_____s occur with great regularity in applied mathematics.

a. Linear equation
b. Quartic equation
c. Difference of two squares
d. Quadratic equation

12. A _____ consists of one quarter of the coordinate plane.
a. 1-center problem
b. 2-3 heap
c. Quadrant
d. 120-cell

13. A _____ is a device for performing mathematical calculations, distinguished from a computer by having a limited problem solving ability and an interface optimized for interactive calculation rather than programming. _____s can be hardware or software, and mechanical or electronic, and are often built into devices such as PDAs or mobile phones.

Modern electronic _____s are generally small, digital, and usually inexpensive.

Chapter 6. INTRODUCTION TO GRAPHING AND STATISTICS

a. 120-cell
b. Calculator
c. 1-center problem
d. 2-3 heap

14. A _____ typically refers to a class of handheld calculators that are capable of plotting graphs, solving simultaneous equations, and performing numerous other tasks with variables. Most popular _____s are also programmable, allowing the user to create customized programs, typically for scientific/engineering and education applications. Due to their large displays intended for graphing, they can also accommodate several lines of text and calculations at a time.

a. Bump mapping
b. Graphing calculator
c. Support vector machines
d. Genus

15. In linear algebra, the _____ of an n-by-n square matrix A is defined to be the sum of the elements on the main diagonal of A. wikimedia.org/math/8/2/b/82be32fa00bd97ebbc066aec3dfe72da.png">

where a_{ij} represents the entry on the ith row and jth column of A. Equivalently, the _____ of a matrix is the sum of its eigenvalues, making it an invariant with respect to a change of basis.

a. Lattice
b. Blinding
c. Constructivism
d. Trace

16. A _____ is an opening in a wall that allows the passage of light and, if not closed or sealed, air and sound. _____s are usually glazed or covered in some other transparent or translucent material. _____s are held in place by frames, which prevent them from collapsing in.

a. 2-3 heap
b. 1-center problem
c. 120-cell
d. Window

17. In mathematics, an _____, or central tendency of a data set refers to a measure of the 'middle' or 'expected' value of the data set. There are many different descriptive statistics that can be chosen as a measurement of the central tendency of the data items.

Chapter 6. INTRODUCTION TO GRAPHING AND STATISTICS

An _____ is a single value that is meant to typify a list of values.

a. A chemical equation
b. A posteriori
c. Average
d. A Mathematical Theory of Communication

18. The term _____ or centre is used in various contexts in abstract algebra to denote the set of all those elements that commute with all other elements. More specifically:

- The _____ of a group G consists of all those elements x in G such that xg = gx for all g in G. This is a normal subgroup of G.
- The _____ of a ring R is the subset of R consisting of all those elements x of R such that xr = rx for all r in R. The _____ is a commutative subring of R, so R is an algebra over its _____.
- The _____ of an algebra A consists of all those elements x of A such that xa = ax for all a in A. See also: central simple algebra.
- The _____ of a Lie algebra L consists of all those elements x in L such that [x,a] = 0 for all a in L. This is an ideal of the Lie algebra L.
- The _____ of a monoidal category C consists of pairs *a natural isomorphism satisfying certain axioms*.

a. Block size
b. Disk
c. Brute Force
d. Center

19. In statistics, _____ has two related meanings:

- the arithmetic _____.
- the expected value of a random variable, which is also called the population _____.

It is sometimes stated that the '_____' _____s average. This is incorrect if '_____' is taken in the specific sense of 'arithmetic _____' as there are different types of averages: the _____, median, and mode. For instance, average house prices almost always use the median value for the average.

For a real-valued random variable X, the _____ is the expectation of X.

a. Probability
b. Proportional hazards model
c. Mean
d. Statistical population

20. A _____ is the result of applying a function to a set of data.

More formally, statistical theory defines a _____ as a function of a sample where the function itself is independent of the sample's distribution: the term is used both for the function and for the value of the function on a given sample.

A _____ is distinct from an unknown statistical parameter, which is not computable from a sample.

a. Parameter space
b. Spatial dependence
c. Loss function
d. Statistic

21. In the physical sciences, _____ is a measurement of the gravitational force acting on an object. Near the surface of the Earth, the acceleration due to gravity is approximately constant; this means that an object's _____ is roughly proportional to its mass.

In commerce and in many other applications, _____ means the same as mass as that term is used in physics.

a. 2-3 heap
b. 1-center problem
c. Weight
d. 120-cell

22. In mathematics, an average, or _____ of a data set refers to a measure of the 'middle' or 'expected' value of the data set. There are many different descriptive statistics that can be chosen as a measurement of the _____ of the data items.

An average is a single value that is meant to typify a list of values.

Chapter 6. INTRODUCTION TO GRAPHING AND STATISTICS

a. Trimean
b. Quartile
c. Central tendency
d. Mean reciprocal rank

23. _____ is a mathematical science pertaining to the collection, analysis, interpretation or explanation, and presentation of data. It also provides tools for prediction and forecasting based on data. It is applicable to a wide variety of academic disciplines, from the natural and social sciences to the humanities, government and business.
    a. Regression toward the mean
    b. Percentile rank
    c. Probability distribution
    d. Statistics

24. In geometry and trigonometry, an _____ is the figure formed by two rays sharing a common endpoint, called the vertex of the _____. The magnitude of the _____ is the 'amount of rotation' that separates the two rays, and can be measured by considering the length of circular arc swept out when one ray is rotated about the vertex to coincide with the other. Where there is no possibility of confusion, the term '_____' is used interchangeably for both the geometric configuration itself and for its angular magnitude.
    a. A posteriori
    b. A Mathematical Theory of Communication
    c. Angle
    d. A chemical equation

25. In geometry, a _____ of a triangle is a line segment joining a vertex to the midpoint of the opposing side. Every triangle has exactly three _____s; one running from each vertex to the opposite side.

The three _____s are concurrent at a point known as the triangle's centroid, or center of mass of the triangle.

a. Percentile rank
b. Correlation
c. Median
d. Statistical significance

26. The _____ is a decimalised system of measurement. It exists in several variations, with different choices of base units, though the choice of base units does not affect its day-to-day use. Over the last two centuries, different variants have been considered the _____.

Chapter 6. INTRODUCTION TO GRAPHING AND STATISTICS

   a. George Dantzig
   b. 1-center problem
   c. Nonlinear system
   d. Metric system

27. In statistics, the _____ is the value that occurs the most frequently in a data set or a probability distribution. In some fields, notably education, sample data are often called scores, and the sample _____ is known as the modal score.

Like the statistical mean and the median, the _____ is a way of capturing important information about a random variable or a population in a single quantity.

   a. Function
   b. Field
   c. Deltoid
   d. Mode

28. _____ is a method of constructing new data points from a discrete set of known data points.
   a. Archimedes' use of infinitesimals
   b. Integration by substitution
   c. Uniform convergence
   d. Interpolation

29. _____ is the likelihood or chance that something is the case or will happen. Theoretical _____ is used extensively in areas such as statistics, mathematics, science and philosophy to draw conclusions about the likelihood of potential events and the underlying mechanics of complex systems.

The word _____ does not have a consistent direct definition.

   a. Probability
   b. Discrete random variable
   c. Standardized moment
   d. Statistical significance

Chapter 7. RATIO AND PROPORTION

1. A _____ is a device for performing mathematical calculations, distinguished from a computer by having a limited problem solving ability and an interface optimized for interactive calculation rather than programming. _____s can be hardware or software, and mechanical or electronic, and are often built into devices such as PDAs or mobile phones.

   Modern electronic _____s are generally small, digital, and usually inexpensive.

   a. 1-center problem
   b. 2-3 heap
   c. 120-cell
   d. Calculator

2. In mathematics the concept of a _____ generalizes notions such as 'length', 'area', and 'volume'. Informally, given some base set, a '_____' is any consistent assignment of 'sizes' to the subsets of the base set. Depending on the application, the 'size' of a subset may be interpreted as its physical size, the amount of something that lies within the subset, or the probability that some random process will yield a result within the subset.

   a. Congruent
   b. Lattice
   c. Cusp
   d. Measure

3. _____ is a special mathematical relationship between two quantities. Two quantities are called proportional if they vary in such a way that one of the quantities is a constant multiple of the other, or equivalently if they have a constant ratio.

   a. Proportionality
   b. Compression
   c. Discontinuity
   d. Depth

4. In mathematics, two quantities are called _____ if they vary in such a way that one of the quantities is a constant multiple of the other, or equivalently if they have a constant ratio.

   a. 2-3 heap
   b. 120-cell
   c. 1-center problem
   d. Proportional

5. In linear algebra, two n-by-n matrices A and B over the field K are called _____ if there exists an invertible n-by-n matrix P over K such that

$$P^{-1}AP = B.$$

Chapter 7. RATIO AND PROPORTION

One of the meanings of the term similarity transformation is such a transformation of a matrix A into a matrix B.

Similarity is an equivalence relation on the space of square matrices.

_____ matrices share many properties:

- rank
- determinant
- trace
- eigenvalues
- characteristic polynomial
- minimal polynomial
- elementary divisors

There are two reasons for these facts:

- two _____ matrices can be thought of as describing the same linear map, but with respect to different bases
- the map $X \mapsto P^{-1}XP$ is an automorphism of the associative algebra of all n-by-n matrices, as the one-object case of the above category of all matrices.

Because of this, for a given matrix A, one is interested in finding a simple 'normal form' B which is _____ to A -- the study of A then reduces to the study of the simpler matrix B.

a. Blinding
b. Coherence
c. Dense
d. Similar

6. A _____ is one of the basic shapes of geometry: a polygon with three corners or vertices and three sides or edges which are line segments. A _____ with vertices A, B, and C is denoted ABC.

In Euclidean geometry any three non-collinear points determine a unique _____ and a unique plane.

a. Triangle
b. 1-center problem
c. Kepler triangle
d. Fuhrmann circle

7.

Chapter 7. RATIO AND PROPORTION

_____ is a Unicode block of 96 symbols at hex codepoint range 25A0-25FF. This range contains various _____.

Only two font sets--Code2000 and the DejaVu family--include coverage for each of the glyphs in the _____ range.

a. 2-3 heap
b. 1-center problem
c. 120-cell
d. Geometric shapes

8. The _____ of an object located in some space refers to the part of space occupied by the object as determined by its external boundary -- abstracting from other aspects the object may have such as its colour, content as well as from the object's position and orientation in space, and its size.

According to famous mathematician and statistician David George Kendall, _____ may be defined as

Simple two-dimensional _____s can be described by basic geometry such as points, line, curves, plane, and so on. _____s that occur in the physical world are often quite complex; they may be arbitrarily curved as studied by differential geometry as for plants or coastlines.)

a. Spidron
b. Parallel lines
c. Shape
d. Confocal

Chapter 8. PERCENT NOTATION

1. A _____ is a device for performing mathematical calculations, distinguished from a computer by having a limited problem solving ability and an interface optimized for interactive calculation rather than programming. _____s can be hardware or software, and mechanical or electronic, and are often built into devices such as PDAs or mobile phones.

Modern electronic _____s are generally small, digital, and usually inexpensive.

   a. 2-3 heap
   b. Calculator
   c. 1-center problem
   d. 120-cell

2. In mathematics the concept of a _____ generalizes notions such as 'length', 'area', and 'volume'. Informally, given some base set, a '_____' is any consistent assignment of 'sizes' to the subsets of the base set. Depending on the application, the 'size' of a subset may be interpreted as its physical size, the amount of something that lies within the subset, or the probability that some random process will yield a result within the subset.
   a. Lattice
   b. Measure
   c. Cusp
   d. Congruent

3. _____ is a special mathematical relationship between two quantities. Two quantities are called proportional if they vary in such a way that one of the quantities is a constant multiple of the other, or equivalently if they have a constant ratio.
   a. Depth
   b. Proportionality
   c. Discontinuity
   d. Compression

4. _____ involves reducing the number of significant digits in a number. The result of _____ is a 'shorter' number having fewer non-zero digits yet similar in magnitude. The result is less precise but easier to use.
   a. Rounding
   b. Hyper operator
   c. Shabakh
   d. Sudan function

5. _____ is a fee, paid on borrowed capital. Assets lent include money, shares, consumer goods through hire purchase, major assets such as aircraft, and even entire factories in finance lease arrangements. The _____ is calculated upon the value of the assets in the same manner as upon money.

a. Interest expense
b. Interest sensitivity gap
c. A Mathematical Theory of Communication
d. Interest

6. In abstract algebra, a module S over a ring R is called _____ or irreducible if it is not the zero module 0 and if its only submodules are 0 and S. Understanding the _____ modules over a ring is usually helpful because these modules form the 'building blocks' of all other modules in a certain sense.

Abelian groups are the same as Z-modules.

a. Derivation
b. Basis
c. Harmonic series
d. Simple

7. _____ is the concept of adding accumulated interest back to the principal, so that interest is earned on interest from that moment on. The act of declaring interest to be principal is called compounding. A loan, for example, may have its interest compounded every month: in this case, a loan with $100 principal and 1% interest per month would have a balance of $101 at the end of the first month.

a. Net interest margin securities
b. Net interest margin
c. Retained interest
d. Compound interest

8. _____ is usually defined as the activity of using and developing computer technology, computer hardware and software. It is the computer-specific part of information technology. Computer science (or _____ science) is the study and the science of the theoretical foundations of information and computation and their implementation and application in computer systems.

a. Deterministic finite state machine
b. Parallel Random Access Machine
c. Probabilistic Turing Machine
d. Computing

Chapter 8. PERCENT NOTATION

9. _____ or amortisation is the process of decreasing an amount over a period of time. The word comes from Middle English amortisen to kill, alienate in mortmain, from Anglo-French amorteser, alteration of amortir, from Vulgar Latin admortire to kill, from Latin ad- + mort-, mors death. Particular instances of the term include:

- _____, the allocation of a lump sum amount to different time periods, particularly for loans and other forms of finance, including related interest or other finance charges.
    - _____ schedule, a table detailing each periodic payment on a loan, as generated by an _____ calculator.
    - Negative _____, an _____ schedule where the loan amount actually increases through not paying the full interest
- Amortized analysis, analyzing the execution cost of algorithms over a sequence of operations.
- _____ of capital expenditures of certain assets under accounting rules, particularly intangible assets, in a manner analogous to depreciation.
- _____

_____ is also used in the context of zoning regulations and describes the time in which a property owner has to relocate when the property's use constitutes a preexisting nonconforming use under zoning regulations.

- Depreciation

a. ISAAC
b. Origin
c. Identity
d. Amortization

Chapter 9. GEOMETRY AND MEASUREMENT

1. _____ is a quantity expressing the two-dimensional size of a defined part of a surface, typically a region bounded by a closed curve. The term surface _____ refers to the total _____ of the exposed surface of a 3-dimensional solid, such as the sum of the _____s of the exposed sides of a polyhedron. _____ is an important invariant in the differential geometry of surfaces.

   a. Area
   b. A posteriori
   c. A Mathematical Theory of Communication
   d. A chemical equation

2. In mathematics the concept of a _____ generalizes notions such as 'length', 'area', and 'volume'. Informally, given some base set, a '_____' is any consistent assignment of 'sizes' to the subsets of the base set. Depending on the application, the 'size' of a subset may be interpreted as its physical size, the amount of something that lies within the subset, or the probability that some random process will yield a result within the subset.

   a. Lattice
   b. Congruent
   c. Cusp
   d. Measure

3. _____ is the mathematical operation of scaling one number by another. It is one of the four basic operations in elementary arithmetic.

   _____ is defined for whole numbers in terms of repeated addition; for example, 4 multiplied by 3 can be calculated by adding 3 copies of 4 together:

   $$4 + 4 + 4 = 12.$$

   _____ of rational numbers and real numbers is defined by systematic generalization of this basic idea.

   a. Least common multiple
   b. The number 0 is even.
   c. Highest common factor
   d. Multiplication

4. In mathematics, _____ is a property that a binary operation can have. It means that, within an expression containing two or more of the same associative operators in a row, the order that the operations are performed does not matter as long as the sequence of the operands is not changed. That is, rearranging the parentheses in such an expression will not change its value.

Chapter 9. GEOMETRY AND MEASUREMENT

a. Algebraically closed
b. Associativity
c. Unital
d. Idempotence

5. The _____ is a decimalised system of measurement. It exists in several variations, with different choices of base units, though the choice of base units does not affect its day-to-day use. Over the last two centuries, different variants have been considered the _____.
a. George Dantzig
b. 1-center problem
c. Metric system
d. Nonlinear system

6. _____ is the measurement of vertical distance, but has two meanings in common use. It can either indicate how 'tall' something is, or how 'high up' it is. For example one could say 'That is a tall building', or 'That airplane is high up in the sky'.
a. 1-center problem
b. Height
c. 2-3 heap
d. 120-cell

7. In geometry, a _____ is a quadrilateral with two sets of parallel sides. The opposite sides of a _____ are of equal length, and the opposite angles of a _____ are congruent. The three-dimensional counterpart of a _____ is a parallelepiped.
a. 1-center problem
b. Parallelogram
c. 2-3 heap
d. 120-cell

8. In mathematics and computer science, _____ (also base-16, hexa or base, of 16. It uses sixteen distinct symbols, most often the symbols 0-9 to represent values zero to nine, and A, B, C, D, E, F (or a through f) to represent values ten to fifteen.

Its primary use is as a human friendly representation of binary coded values, so it is often used in digital electronics and computer engineering.

Chapter 9. GEOMETRY AND MEASUREMENT

   a. Hexadecimal
   b. Factoradic
   c. Radix
   d. Tetradecimal

9. A _____ or a trapezium is a quadrilateral that has at least one pair of parallel lines for sides.

Some authors define it as a quadrilateral having exactly one pair of parallel sides, so as to exclude parallelograms, which otherwise would be regarded as a special type of _____, but most mathematicians use the inclusive definition.

In North America, the term trapezium is used to refer to a quadrilateral with no parallel sides.

   a. Trapezium
   b. Trapezoid
   c. Lozenge
   d. Rhomboid

10. Scientific notation, also sometimes known as standard form or as _____, is a way of writing numbers that accommodates values too large or small to be conveniently written in standard decimal notation. Scientific notation has a number of useful properties and is often favored by scientists, mathematicians and engineers, who work with such numbers.

In scientific notation, numbers are written in the form:

$$a \times 10^b$$

   a. Exponential notation
   b. A Mathematical Theory of Communication
   c. A chemical equation
   d. A posteriori

11. A _____ is a simple shape of Euclidean geometry consisting of those points in a plane which are at a constant distance, called the radius, from a fixed point, called the center. A _____ with center A is sometimes denoted by the symbol A.

A chord of a _____ is a line segment whose two endpoints lie on the _____.

a. Circle
b. Circumcircle
c. Circular segment
d. Malfatti circles

12. In classical geometry, a _____ of a circle or sphere is any line segment from its center to its boundary. By extension, the _____ of a circle or sphere is the length of any such segment. The _____ is half the diameter. In science and engineering the term _____ of curvature is commonly used as a synonym for _____.

a. Non-Euclidean geometry
b. Birational geometry
c. Duoprism
d. Radius

13. The _____ is the distance around a closed curve. _____ is a kind of perimeter.

The _____ of a circle is the length around it.

a. Brascamp-Lieb inequality
b. Compactness measure of a shape
c. Flatness
d. Circumference

14. A _____ is a device for performing mathematical calculations, distinguished from a computer by having a limited problem solving ability and an interface optimized for interactive calculation rather than programming. _____s can be hardware or software, and mechanical or electronic, and are often built into devices such as PDAs or mobile phones.

Modern electronic _____s are generally small, digital, and usually inexpensive.

a. 120-cell
b. 2-3 heap
c. 1-center problem
d. Calculator

15. The _____ of any solid, plasma, vacuum or theoretical object is how much three-dimensional space it occupies, often quantified numerically. One-dimensional figures and two-dimensional shapes are assigned zero _____ in the three-dimensional space. _____ is presented as ml or cm^3.

_____s of straight-edged and circular shapes are calculated using arithmetic formulae.

a. Thermodynamic limit
b. Cauchy momentum equation
c. Stress-energy tensor
d. Volume

16. In mathematics, the _____s are analogs of the ordinary trigonometric functions. The basic _____s are the hyperbolic sine 'sinh', and the hyperbolic cosine 'cosh', from which are derived the hyperbolic tangent 'tanh', etc., in analogy to the derived trigonometric functions. The inverse _____ are the area hyperbolic sine 'arsinh' (also called 'asinh', or sometimes by the misnomer of 'arcsinh') and so on.
   a. Hyperbolic function
   b. Rectangular function
   c. Square root
   d. Heaviside step function

17. In common usage, a cylinder is taken to mean a finite section of a right _____ with its ends closed to form two circular surfaces, as in the figure (right.) If the cylinder has a radius r and length (height) h, then its volume is given by

$$V = \pi r^2 h$$

and its surface area is:

- the area of the top (πr^2) +
- the area of the bottom (πr^2) +
- the area of the side $(2\pi r h)$.

Therefore without the top or bottom (lateral area), the surface area is

$$A = 2\pi r h.$$

With the top and bottom, the surface area is

$$A = 2\pi r^2 + 2\pi r h = 2\pi r(r + h).$$

For a given volume, the cylinder with the smallest surface area has h = 2r. For a given surface area, the cylinder with the largest volume has h = 2r, i.e. the cylinder fits in a cube (height = diameter.)

Cylindric sections are the intersections of cylinders with planes.

Chapter 9. GEOMETRY AND MEASUREMENT

  a. 1-center problem
  b. Circular cylinder
  c. 2-3 heap
  d. 120-cell

18. In mathematics, a _____ is a quadric surface, with the following equation in Cartesian coordinates: $(x/_a)^2 + (y/_b)^2 = 1$.
  a. Derivative algebra
  b. Free
  c. Cylinder
  d. Discontinuity

19. A _____ is a symmetrical geometrical object. In non-mathematical usage, the term is used to refer either to a round ball or to its two-dimensional surface. In mathematics, a _____ is the set of all points in three-dimensional space which are at distance r from a fixed point of that space, where r is a positive real number called the radius of the _____.
  a. Differentiable manifold
  b. Sphere
  c. Differential geometry of curves
  d. Lie derivative

20. The x-axis is the horizontal axis of a two- dimensional plot in the _____, that is typically pointed to the right. Also known as a right-handed coordinate system.
  a. Cartesian coordinate system
  b. 1-center problem
  c. 2-3 heap
  d. 120-cell

21. In geometry and trigonometry, an _____ is the figure formed by two rays sharing a common endpoint, called the vertex of the _____. The magnitude of the _____ is the 'amount of rotation' that separates the two rays, and can be measured by considering the length of circular arc swept out when one ray is rotated about the vertex to coincide with the other. Where there is no possibility of confusion, the term '_____' is used interchangeably for both the geometric configuration itself and for its angular magnitude.
  a. A chemical equation
  b. A Mathematical Theory of Communication
  c. A posteriori
  d. Angle

Chapter 9. GEOMETRY AND MEASUREMENT

22. In geometry, a _____ is a special kind of point, usually a corner of a polygon, polyhedron, or higher dimensional polytope. In the geometry of curves a _____ is a point of where the first derivative of curvature is zero. In graph theory, a _____ is the fundamental unit out of which graphs are formed
    a. Duality
    b. Dini
    c. Vertex
    d. Crib

23. An angle smaller than a right angle is called an _____ (less than 90 degrees).
    a. Euclidean geometry
    b. Ultraparallel theorem
    c. Integral geometry
    d. Acute angle

24. In mathematics, the _____ of a number n is the number that, when added to n, yields zero. The _____ of n is denoted −n. For example, 7 is −7, because 7 + (−7) = 0, and the _____ of −0.3 is 0.3, because −0.3 + 0.3 = 0.
    a. Algebraic structure
    b. Associativity
    c. Arity
    d. Additive inverse

25. In geometry and trigonometry, a _____ is defined as an angle between two straight intersecting lines of ninety degrees, or one-quarter of a circle.
    a. Right angle
    b. Trigonometric functions
    c. Sine integral
    d. Trigonometry

26. An angle equal to two right angles is called a _____ (equal to 180 degrees).
    a. Householder transformation
    b. Loomis-Whitney inequality
    c. Theorem
    d. Straight angle

27. A pair of angles are said to be _____ if they share the same vertex and are bounded by the same pair of lines but are opposite to each other. They are also congruent.

Chapter 9. GEOMETRY AND MEASUREMENT

a. Line segment
b. Hinge theorem
c. Vertical angles
d. Reflection symmetry

28. In discrete mathematics and predominantly in set theory, a _____ is a concept used in comparisons of sets to refer to the unique values of one set in relation to another. The terms 'absolute' and 'relative' _____ refer to more specific applications of the concept, with universal _____s referring to elements unique to the universal set and the latter referring to the unique elements of one set in relation to another. In this image, the universal set is represented by the border of the image, and the set A as a disc.

a. Derivative algebra
b. Kernel
c. Huge
d. Complement

29. A pair of angles are complementary if the sum of their measures add up to 90 degrees.

If the two _____ are adjacent (i.e. have a common vertex and share a side, but do not have any interior points in common) their non-shared sides form a right angle.

In Euclidean geometry, the two acute angles in a right triangle are complementary, because there are 180>° in a triangle and 90>° have been accounted for by the right angle.

a. Conway polyhedron notation
b. Complementary angles
c. Hypotenuse
d. Quincunx

30. A pair of angles is _____ if their measurements add up to 180 degrees. If the two _____ angles are adjacent their non-shared sides form a straight line. The supplement of 135 would be 45.

a. Cylinder
b. Supplementary
c. FISH
d. Dense

31. In geometry, an _____ is a triangle in which all three sides have equal lengths. In traditional or Euclidean geometry, _____s are also equiangular; that is, all three internal angles are also equal to each other and are each 60°. They are regular polygons, and can therefore also be referred to as regular triangles.

Chapter 9. GEOMETRY AND MEASUREMENT

a. A chemical equation
b. A Mathematical Theory of Communication
c. Isotomic conjugate
d. Equilateral triangle

32. An _____ is a triangle that has one internal angle larger than 90°
a. A Mathematical Theory of Communication
b. Obtuse triangle
c. A chemical equation
d. Isotomic conjugate

33. A _____ is one of the basic shapes of geometry: a polygon with three corners or vertices and three sides or edges which are line segments. A _____ with vertices A, B, and C is denoted ABC.

In Euclidean geometry any three non-collinear points determine a unique _____ and a unique plane.

a. Fuhrmann circle
b. Kepler triangle
c. Triangle
d. 1-center problem

34. In mathematics, an algebraic group G contains a unique maximal normal solvable subgroup; and this subgroup is closed. Its identity component is called the _____ of G.
a. Barycentric coordinates
b. Composite
c. Radical
d. Block size

35. In mathematics, a _____ of a number x is a number r such that r^2 = x, or, in other words, a number r whose square is x. Every non-negative real number x has a unique non-negative _____, called the principal _____, which is denoted with a radical symbol as $\sqrt{x}$, or, using exponent notation, as $x^{1/2}$. For example, the principal _____ of 9 is 3, denoted $\sqrt{9}$ = 3, because 3^2 = 3 × 3 = 9.

Chapter 9. GEOMETRY AND MEASUREMENT

a. Multiplicative inverse
b. Hyperbolic functions
c. Double exponential
d. Square root

36. In vascular plants, the _____ is the organ of a plant body that typically lies below the surface of the soil. This is not always the case, however, since a _____ can also be aerial (that is, growing above the ground) or aerating (that is, growing up above the ground or especially above water.) Furthermore, a stem normally occurring below ground is not exceptional either

a. Root
b. 1-center problem
c. 120-cell
d. 2-3 heap

37. A _____ is the longest side of a right triangle, the side opposite of the right angle. The length of the _____ of a right triangle can be found using the Pythagorean theorem, which states that the square of the length of the _____ equals the sum of the squares of the lengths of the two other sides.

For example, if one of the other sides has a length of 3 meters and the other has a length of 4 m.

a. Golden angle
b. Hypotenuse
c. Reflection symmetry
d. Concyclic points

38. In a right triangle, the cathetusoriginally from the Greek word Κἲ¬θετος, plural catheti

- 1 Generally
- 2 References
- 3 See also
- 4 External links

In a wider sense, a _____ is any line falling perpendicularly on another line or a surface. Such a line is more commonly known as a surface normal.

a. Cathetus
b. Central angle
c. Face diagonal
d. Line segment

39. In mathematics, the _____ or Pythagoras' theorem is a relation in Euclidean geometry among the three sides of a right triangle. The theorem is named after the Greek mathematician Pythagoras, who by tradition is credited with its discovery and proof, although it is often argued that knowledge of the theory predates him.. The theorem is as follows:

In any right triangle, the area of the square whose side is the hypotenuse is equal to the sum of the areas of the squares whose sides are the two legs.

a. 2-3 heap
b. 1-center problem
c. 120-cell
d. Pythagorean theorem

40. In mathematics, a _____ is a statement that can be proved on the basis of explicitly stated or previously agreed assumptions.
a. Logical value
b. Disjunction introduction
c. Boolean function
d. Theorem

41. In the physical sciences, _____ is a measurement of the gravitational force acting on an object. Near the surface of the Earth, the acceleration due to gravity is approximately constant; this means that an object's _____ is roughly proportional to its mass.

In commerce and in many other applications, _____ means the same as mass as that term is used in physics.

a. 120-cell
b. 2-3 heap
c. Weight
d. 1-center problem

42. _____ is a temperature scale that is named after the German physicist Daniel Gabriel _____, who proposed it in 1724.

Chapter 9. GEOMETRY AND MEASUREMENT

In this scale, the freezing point of water is 32 degrees _____ and the boiling point 212 °F, placing the boiling and freezing points of water exactly 180 degrees apart. A degree on the _____ scale is 1/180th part of the interval between the ice point and the boiling point.

a. 2-3 heap
b. 120-cell
c. Fahrenheit
d. 1-center problem

43. A _____ is a software program that facilitates symbolic mathematics. The core functionality of a CAS is manipulation of mathematical expressions in symbolic form.

The symbolic manipulations supported typically include

- simplification to the smallest possible expression or some standard form, including automatic simplification with assumptions and simplification with constraints
- substitution of symbolic, functors or numeric values for expressions
- change of form of expressions: expanding products and powers, partial and full factorization, rewriting as partial fractions, constraint satisfaction, rewriting trigonometric functions as exponentials, etc.
- partial and total differentiation
- symbolic constrained and unconstrained global optimization
- solution of linear and some non-linear equations over various domains
- solution of some differential and difference equations
- taking some limits
- some indefinite and definite integration, including multidimensional integrals
- integral transforms
- arbitrary-precision numeric operations
- Series operations such as expansion, summation and products
- matrix operations including products, inverses, etc.
- display of mathematical expressions in two-dimensional mathematical form, often using typesetting systems similar to TeX
- add-ons for use in applied mathematics such as physics packages for physical computation
- plotting graphs and parametric plots of functions in two and three dimensions, and animating them
- APIs for linking it on an external program such as a database, or using in a programming language to use the _____
- drawing charts and diagrams
- string manipulation such as matching and searching
- statistical computation
- Theorem proving and verification
- graphic production and editing such as CGI and signal processing as image processing
- sound synthesis

Chapter 9. GEOMETRY AND MEASUREMENT

Many also include a programming language, allowing users to implement their own algorithms.

Some _____s focus on a specific area of application; these are typically developed in academia and are free.

a. Computer algebra system
b. 2-3 heap
c. 120-cell
d. 1-center problem

Chapter 10. POLYNOMIALS

1. In mathematics, the word _____ means two different things in the context of polynomials:

   - The first meaning is a product of powers of variables, or formally any value obtained from 1 by finitely many multiplications by a variable. If only a single variable x is considered this means that any _____ is either 1 or a power x^n of x, with n a positive integer. If several variables are considered, say, x, y, z, then each can be given an exponent, so that any _____ is of the form $x^a y^b z^c$ with a,b,c nonnegative integers.
   - The second meaning of _____ includes _____s in the first sense, but also allows multiplication by any constant, so that − $7x^5$ and $4yz^{13}$ are also considered to be _____s.

   With either definition, the set of _____s is a subset of all polynomials that is closed under multiplication.

   a. Monomial
   b. Homogeneous polynomial
   c. Power sum symmetric polynomial
   d. Diagonal form

2. In mathematics, a _____ is an expression constructed from variables and constants, using the operations of addition, subtraction, multiplication, and constant non-negative whole number exponents. For example, $x^2 - 4x + 7$ is a _____, but $x^2 - 4/x + 7x^{3/2}$ is not, because its second term involves division by the variable x and also because its third term contains an exponent that is not a whole number.

   _____s are one of the most important concepts in algebra and throughout mathematics and science.

   a. Group extension
   b. Semifield
   c. Coimage
   d. Polynomial

3. An _____ is a number which is involved in addition. A number being added is considered to be an _____.
   a. A chemical equation
   b. A posteriori
   c. A Mathematical Theory of Communication
   d. Addend

4. In mathematics, the _____ of a number n is the number that, when added to n, yields zero. The _____ of n is denoted −n. For example, 7 is −7, because 7 + (−7) = 0, and the _____ of −0.3 is 0.3, because −0.3 + 0.3 = 0.

a. Associativity
b. Algebraic structure
c. Additive inverse
d. Arity

5. The _____ is a rule which states that when you add or multiply numbers, changing the order doesn't change the result.
a. Coimage
b. Semigroupoid
c. Conditional event algebra
d. Commutative law

6. In mathematics, an _____ in the sense of ring theory is a subring $\mathcal{O}$ of a ring R that satisfies the conditions

   1. R is a ring which is a finite-dimensional algebra over the rational number field $\mathbb{Q}$
   2. $\mathcal{O}$ spans R over $\mathbb{Q}$, so that $\mathbb{Q}\mathcal{O} = R$, and
   3. $\mathcal{O}$ is a lattice in R.

The third condition can be stated more accurately, in terms of the extension of scalars of R to the real numbers, embedding R in a real vector space. In less formal terms, additively $\mathcal{O}$ should be a free abelian group generated by a basis for R over $\mathbb{Q}$.

The leading example is the case where R is a number field K and $\mathcal{O}$ is its ring of integers. In algebraic number theory there are examples for any K other than the rational field of proper subrings of the ring of integers that are also _____s.

a. Algebraic
b. Efficiency
c. Annihilator
d. Order

7. In abstract algebra, a field extension L/K is called _____ if every element of L is _____ over K. Field extensions which are not _____.

For example, the field extension R/Q, that is the field of real numbers as an extension of the field of rational numbers, is transcendental, while the field extensions C/R and Q

a. Identity
b. Algebraic
c. Echo
d. Ideal

8. A _____ is a software program that facilitates symbolic mathematics. The core functionality of a CAS is manipulation of mathematical expressions in symbolic form.

The symbolic manipulations supported typically include

- simplification to the smallest possible expression or some standard form, including automatic simplification with assumptions and simplification with constraints
- substitution of symbolic, functors or numeric values for expressions
- change of form of expressions: expanding products and powers, partial and full factorization, rewriting as partial fractions, constraint satisfaction, rewriting trigonometric functions as exponentials, etc.
- partial and total differentiation
- symbolic constrained and unconstrained global optimization
- solution of linear and some non-linear equations over various domains
- solution of some differential and difference equations
- taking some limits
- some indefinite and definite integration, including multidimensional integrals
- integral transforms
- arbitrary-precision numeric operations
- Series operations such as expansion, summation and products
- matrix operations including products, inverses, etc.
- display of mathematical expressions in two-dimensional mathematical form, often using typesetting systems similar to TeX
- add-ons for use in applied mathematics such as physics packages for physical computation
- plotting graphs and parametric plots of functions in two and three dimensions, and animating them
- APIs for linking it on an external program such as a database, or using in a programming language to use the _____
- drawing charts and diagrams
- string manipulation such as matching and searching
- statistical computation
- Theorem proving and verification
- graphic production and editing such as CGI and signal processing as image processing
- sound synthesis

Many also include a programming language, allowing users to implement their own algorithms.

Some _____s focus on a specific area of application; these are typically developed in academia and are free.

Chapter 10. POLYNOMIALS

a. 2-3 heap
b. 1-center problem
c. 120-cell
d. Computer algebra system

9. _____ is the mathematical operation of scaling one number by another. It is one of the four basic operations in elementary arithmetic.

_____ is defined for whole numbers in terms of repeated addition; for example, 4 multiplied by 3 can be calculated by adding 3 copies of 4 together:

$$4 + 4 + 4 = 12.$$

_____ of rational numbers and real numbers is defined by systematic generalization of this basic idea.

a. Highest common factor
b. Multiplication
c. Least common multiple
d. The number 0 is even.

10. In mathematics, _____ is a property that a binary operation can have. It means that, within an expression containing two or more of the same associative operators in a row, the order that the operations are performed does not matter as long as the sequence of the operands is not changed. That is, rearranging the parentheses in such an expression will not change its value.

a. Unital
b. Idempotence
c. Algebraically closed
d. Associativity

11. Exponentiation is a mathematical operation, written a^n, involving two numbers, the base a and the _____ n. When n is a positive integer, exponentiation corresponds to repeated multiplication:

$$a^n = \underbrace{a \times \cdots \times a}_{n},$$

just as multiplication by a positive integer corresponds to repeated addition:

$$a \times n = \underbrace{a + \cdots + a}_{n}.$$

The _____ is usually shown as a superscript to the right of the base. The exponentiation a^n can be read as: a raised to the n-th power, a raised to the power [of] n or possibly a raised to the _____ [of] n, or more briefly: a to the n-th power or a to the power [of] n, or even more briefly: a to the n.

  a. Exponential tree
  b. Exponent
  c. Exponential sum
  d. Exponentiating by squaring

12. Scientific notation, also sometimes known as standard form or as _____, is a way of writing numbers that accommodates values too large or small to be conveniently written in standard decimal notation. Scientific notation has a number of useful properties and is often favored by scientists, mathematicians and engineers, who work with such numbers.

In scientific notation, numbers are written in the form:

$$a \times 10^b$$

  a. A chemical equation
  b. A Mathematical Theory of Communication
  c. A posteriori
  d. Exponential notation

13. The _____ governs the differentiation of products of differentiable functions.
  a. 1-center problem
  b. 120-cell
  c. Reciprocal Rule
  d. Product rule

14. In elementary algebra, a _____ is a polynomial with two terms: the sum of two monomials. It is the simplest kind of polynomial except for a monomial.

Chapter 10. POLYNOMIALS

The _____ $a^2 - b^2$ can be factored as the product of two other _____s:

$a^2 - b^2$.

The product of a pair of linear _____s $ax + b$ and $cx + d$ is:

$2 + x + bd$.

A _____ raised to the nth power, represented as

n

can be expanded by means of the _____ theorem or, equivalently, using Pascal's triangle.

a. Rational root theorem
b. Real structure
c. Cylindrical algebraic decomposition
d. Binomial

15. In mathematics, and in particular in abstract algebra, distributivity is a property of binary operations that generalises the _____ law from elementary algebra.
    a. Permutation
    b. General linear group
    c. Closure with a twist
    d. Distributive

16. In elementary algebra, a _____ is a polynomial consisting of three terms; in other words, a _____ is the sum of three monomials. It can be factored using simple steps

In linguistics, a _____ is a fixed expression which is made from three words; e.g. 'lights, camera, action', 'signed, sealed, delivered'.

a. Relation algebra
b. Recurrence relation
c. Symmetric difference
d. Trinomial

Chapter 10. POLYNOMIALS

17. _____, also sometimes known as standard form or as exponential notation, is a way of writing numbers that accommodates values too large or small to be conveniently written in standard decimal notation. _____ has a number of useful properties and is often favored by scientists, mathematicians and engineers, who work with such numbers.

In _____, numbers are written in the form:

$$a \times 10^b$$

    a. 1-center problem
    b. Scientific notation
    c. Radix point
    d. Leading zero

18. The _____ are the set of numbers consisting of the natural numbers including 0 and their negatives. They are numbers that can be written without a fractional or decimal component, and fall within the set {... −2, −1, 0, 1, 2, ...}.
    a. A Mathematical Theory of Communication
    b. A posteriori
    c. A chemical equation
    d. Integers

19. A _____ is a device for performing mathematical calculations, distinguished from a computer by having a limited problem solving ability and an interface optimized for interactive calculation rather than programming. _____s can be hardware or software, and mechanical or electronic, and are often built into devices such as PDAs or mobile phones.

Modern electronic _____s are generally small, digital, and usually inexpensive.

    a. 120-cell
    b. 2-3 heap
    c. Calculator
    d. 1-center problem

20. In mathematics the concept of a _____ generalizes notions such as 'length', 'area', and 'volume'. Informally, given some base set, a '_____' is any consistent assignment of 'sizes' to the subsets of the base set. Depending on the application, the 'size' of a subset may be interpreted as its physical size, the amount of something that lies within the subset, or the probability that some random process will yield a result within the subset.

Chapter 10. POLYNOMIALS

a. Lattice
b. Congruent
c. Cusp
d. Measure

21. In mathematics the _____ of a set which is equipped with the operation of addition is an element which, when added to any element x in the set, yields x. One of the most familiar additive identities is the number 0 from elementary mathematics, but additive identities occur in other mathematical structures where addition is defined, such as in groups and rings.

- The _____ familiar from elementary mathematics is zero, denoted 0. For example,

    5 + 0 = 5 = 0 + 5.

- In the natural numbers N and all of its supersets, the _____ is 0. Thus for any one of these numbers n,

    n + 0 = n = 0 + n.

Let N be a set which is closed under the operation of addition, denoted +. An _____ for N is any element e such that for any element n in N,

e + n = n = n + e.

a. Algebraically independent
b. Unit ring
c. Unique factorization domain
d. Additive identity

22. In mathematics, the term _____ has several different important meanings:

- An _____ is an equality that remains true regardless of the values of any variables that appear within it, to distinguish it from an equality which is true under more particular conditions. For this, the 'triple bar' symbol ≡ is sometimes used.
- In algebra, an _____ or _____ element of a set S with a binary operation · is an element e that, when combined with any element x of S, produces that same x. That is, e·x = x·e = x for all x in S.
    - The _____ function from a set S to itself, often denoted id or id_S, s the function such that i = x for all x in S. This function serves as the _____ element in the set of all functions from S to itself with respect to function composition.
    - In linear algebra, the _____ matrix of size n is the n-by-n square matrix with ones on the main diagonal and zeros elsewhere. This matrix serves as the _____ with respect to matrix multiplication.

Chapter 10. POLYNOMIALS

A common example of the first meaning is the trigonometric _____

$$\sin^2 \theta + \cos^2 \theta = 1$$

which is true for all real values of θ, as opposed to

$$\cos \theta = 1,$$

which is true only for some values of θ, not all. For example, the latter equation is true when $\theta = 0$, false when $\theta = 2$

The concepts of 'additive _____' and 'multiplicative _____' are central to the Peano axioms. The number 0 is the 'additive _____' for integers, real numbers, and complex numbers. For the real numbers, for all $a \in \mathbb{R}$,

$$0 + a = a,$$

$$a + 0 = a, \text{ and}$$

$$0 + 0 = 0.$$

Similarly, The number 1 is the 'multiplicative _____' for integers, real numbers, and complex numbers.

a. Intersection
b. Action
c. ARIA
d. Identity

23. In mathematics, a _____ can mean either an element of the set {1, 2, 3, ...} (i.e the positive integers) or an element of the set {0, 1, 2, 3, ...} (i.e. the non-negative integers).
a. Whole number
b. FISH
c. Bounded
d. Degrees of freedom

24. In mathematics, a division is called a _____ if the divisor is zero. Such a division can be formally expressed as $\frac{a}{0}$ where a is the dividend. Whether this expression can be assigned a well-defined value depends upon the mathematical setting.

a. 1-center problem
b. Division by Zero
c. 2-3 heap
d. 120-cell

25. In mathematics, a _____ is the end result of a division problem. It can also be expressed as the number of times the divisor divides into the dividend.
a. Quotient
b. Notation
c. Marginal cost
d. Limiting

ANSWER KEY

Chapter 1
1. d	2. d	3. a	4. d	5. a	6. d	7. c	8. d	9. b	10. b
11. a	12. a	13. b	14. b	15. c	16. c	17. d	18. d	19. d	20. d
21. b	22. d	23. d	24. b	25. c	26. b	27. d	28. b	29. d	30. d
31. c	32. d	33. c	34. d	35. d	36. b	37. a	38. d	39. d	40. c

Chapter 2
1. a	2. d	3. d	4. d	5. b	6. b	7. d	8. d	9. d	10. d
11. a	12. d	13. d	14. d	15. d	16. b	17. d	18. d	19. a	20. b
21. d	22. d	23. d	24. a	25. d	26. c	27. d			

Chapter 3
1. d	2. d	3. d	4. d	5. c	6. d	7. d	8. c	9. d	10. c
11. c	12. a	13. a	14. d	15. d	16. a	17. d	18. a	19. d	20. d
21. d	22. d	23. d	24. c	25. d	26. d	27. d	28. a		

Chapter 4
1. d	2. d	3. a	4. c	5. d	6. d	7. d	8. d	9. d	10. c
11. d	12. a	13. d	14. d	15. a	16. d				

Chapter 5
1. d	2. d	3. d	4. d	5. b	6. b	7. d	8. d	9. a	10. d
11. c	12. c	13. c	14. d	15. d	16. d	17. d	18. c	19. d	20. b
21. d	22. b								

Chapter 6
1. d	2. d	3. d	4. c	5. d	6. d	7. a	8. a	9. c	10. d
11. a	12. c	13. b	14. b	15. d	16. d	17. c	18. d	19. c	20. d
21. c	22. c	23. d	24. c	25. c	26. d	27. d	28. d	29. a	

Chapter 7
1. d	2. d	3. a	4. d	5. d	6. a	7. d	8. c

Chapter 8
1. b	2. b	3. b	4. a	5. d	6. d	7. d	8. d	9. d

Chapter 9
1. a	2. d	3. d	4. b	5. c	6. b	7. b	8. a	9. b	10. a
11. a	12. d	13. d	14. d	15. d	16. a	17. b	18. c	19. b	20. a
21. d	22. c	23. d	24. d	25. a	26. d	27. c	28. d	29. b	30. b
31. d	32. b	33. c	34. c	35. d	36. a	37. b	38. a	39. d	40. d
41. c	42. c	43. a							

ANSWER KEY

Chapter 10
1. a   2. d   3. d   4. c   5. d   6. d   7. b   8. d   9. b   10. d
11. b   12. d   13. d   14. d   15. d   16. d   17. b   18. d   19. c   20. d
21. d   22. d   23. a   24. b   25. a

www.ingramcontent.com/pod-product-compliance
Lightning Source LLC
Chambersburg PA
CBHW081848230426
43669CB00018B/2872